CHARMING SMALL HOTEL GUIDES

Venice

& North-East Italy

CHARMING SMALL HOTEL GUIDES

Venice

& North-East Italy

Edited by

Fiona Duncan and Leonie Glass

Conceived, designed and produced by
Duncan Petersen Publishing Ltd

Editorial Director   Andrew Duncan
Production Editor   Nicola Davies
Art Director   Mel Petersen
Designers   Christopher Foley
                         Beverley Stewart
Maps   Christopher Foley

This edition published 1998 by
Duncan Petersen Publishing Ltd,
31 Ceylon Road, London W14 OPY

Sales representation in the UK and Ireland by
World Leisure Marketing,
9 Downing Road, West Meadows Industrial Estate,
Derby DE21 6HA

Distributed by **Grantham Book Services**

ISBN 1 872576 75 3

A CIP catalogue record for this book is available
from the British Library

AND

Published in the USA by
Hunter Publishing Inc.,
130 Campus Drive, Edison, N.J. 08818.
Tel (732) 225 1900 Fax (732) 417 0482

ISBN 1-55650-828-X

Typeset by Duncan Petersen Publishing Ltd
Printed in Spain by G Z Printek

Contents

This is the second Italian regional guide in Duncan Petersen's *Charming Small Hotel Guides* series. It follows the success of the first, *Tuscany & Umbria.*

That book, we have learned from readers' letters, appealed especially to enthusiasts who are regular visitors to Italy. They appreciate its in-depth approach, providing many new ideas for places to stay which for reasons of space our long-established all-Italy guide cannot supply.

This new guide offers the same in-depth approach: it is no mere rehash of the all-Italy guide, but contains a wealth of new entries; some are new discoveries, never published before. They include not just hotels, from humble to luxurious, but also guest houses (*pensioni*), farmhouse bed-and-breakfasts (*agriturismo*) and self-catering accommodation that has our special qualities of character and charm.

If you already know Venice and North-East Italy, and are revisiting, this guide will refuel your enthusiasm. If you are going for the first time, it is essential reading.

Venice and North-East Italy for the traveller
Venice hardly needs any introduction, famed as it is throughout the world as a city of incomparable beauty, romance and artistic wealth. Built on mudbanks which extend into the tidal waters of the Adriatic where East meets West, Venice was once a great maritime power ruled by its doges, and a place of plot, intrigue and decadence. A city of water and of light, with an atmosphere which is at once fascinating and disturbing, its fragile fabric of canals and *palazzi*, churches, alleyways and *campi* has somehow survived the threats of both flood and mass tourism, and remarkably little has changed throughout the centuries. Nowhere in Venice will you see an ugly sight; even the Macdonalds near the Rialto is just about bearable. At any time of the year you can escape the crowds of tourists who throng Piazza San Marco, the Rialto and the main thoroughfare between the two by simply slipping into the backstreets where there is always a church, a canal, a café to divert you; the best time to visit, however, is in spring and early summer or autumn, when the crowds are thinner and the weather can be lovely. During 1997, for example, there was a long spell of warm weather and blue skies in March, while June was often wet and overcast.

Stretching inland from Venice in a great arc as far as the Austrian border to the north and the shores of Lake Garda to the west is the province of Veneto. While the landscape of the vast Veneto Plain which fans out behind Venice is largely industrialized and pancake flat (save for the green Euganean Hills and Berici Mountains), it is full of interest. The great cities of Padua, Treviso, Vicenza and Verona are time-consuming enough, but then there are the villas of Palladio and other attractions such as the charming little towns of Asolo and Montagnana. To the west of Venice, the Plain edges into the province of Friuli-Venezia Giulia, curving round the coastline towards Trieste and the border with Slovenia and, to the north, reaching into the high Alps and the border with Austria.

The presence of the mountains gives this guide a rich flavour and makes the range of accommodation contained in it, from Venetian *palazzo* to Tyrolean chalet, wonderfully varied. The mainly mountainous province of Trentino-Alto Adige, which stretches north from Lake Garda, feels a million miles away from Venice. As the mountains rise towards the Austrian border, so the distinction between the two countries becomes blurred. Here in this northernmost region of Italy, also known as Southern Tyrol, you will find that the people are German-speaking (all the place names have both German and Italian translations) and that they share the same culture and traditions as their neighbours over the border. The hospitality is warm, the scenery is breathtakingly beautiful, often with the jagged peaks of the Dolomites serving as a dramatic backdrop. In winter you can ski and in summer you can walk. It would be hard to imagine a more delightful and varied holiday than to start in the Southern Tyrol, descend to the serene shores of Lake Garda (in this guide we include the western shore which falls into the province of Lombardia), then cut across the Veneto Plain taking in Verona, Vicenza, Padua, and finally reach the greatest glory of all, Venice itself. You will not lack for lovely places to stay along the way, and with this guide you can plan the perfect trip.

Our criteria
Although this guide covers a much smaller territory than the majority of guides in the series, the selection criteria remains the same. We aim to include only those places that are in some way captivating, with a distinctive personality, and which offer a truly personal service. In Venice especially we wanted to give as broad a range of recommendations as possible, to suit all budgets, as hotels are often fully booked and you may need several alternatives to your first choice, especially if travelling at short notice. We found many hotels here which easily attain our very high standards; but there are a significant number, which, though basically recommendable, for one reason or another fall short of our ideal. The descriptions of each hotel make this distinction clear. Be assured that all the hotels in the guide are, one way or another, true to the concept of the charming small hotel, and that they are the pick of the dozens of small hotels in Venice. If you find any more, please let us know (see page 32).

In making our selection, we have been careful to bear in mind the many different requirements of our readers. Some will be backpackers; others will be millionaires; the vast majority will fall between the two. They all have in common their preference for a small, intimate hotel rather than a large anonymous one. Whether the hotel be a one-star hostel or a four-star *palazzo*, it has been included because it fulfils our crieria.

Charming and small
Ideally the hotel will have less than 30 bedrooms; but this is not a rigid requirement – many hotels with more than 30 bedrooms feel much smaller, and you will find such places in this guide. We attach more importance to size than other guides because we think that unless a hotel is small, it cannot give a genuinely personal welcome, or make you feel like an individual, rather than just a guest. Unlike other guides, we often rule out places that have great qualities, but are nonetheless no more nor less than – hotels. Our hotels are all special in some way.

We think that we have a much clearer idea than other guides of what is special and what is not; and we think we apply these criteria more consistently than other guides because we are a small and personally managed company rather than a bureaucracy. We have a small team of like-minded inspectors, thoroughly rehearsed in recognizing what we want. While we very much appreciate readers' reports – see below – they are not our main source of information.

So what exactly do we look for?
- A calm, attractive setting in an interesting and picturesque position.
- A building that is either handsome or interesting or historic, or at least with a distinct character.
- Bedrooms which are well proportioned with as much character as the public rooms below.
- Ideally, we look for adequate space, but on a human scale: we don't go for places that rely on grandeur, or that have pretensions that could intimidate.
- Decorations must be harmonious and in good taste, and the furnishings and facilities comfortable and well maintained. We like to see interesting antique furniture that is there because it can be used, not simply revered.
- The proprietors and staff need to be dedicated and thoughtful, offering a personal welcome, *without being intrusive.* The guest needs to feel like an individual.

Whole-page entries
We rarely see all these qualities together in one place; but our warmest recommendations – whole page, with photograph – usually lack only one or two of these qualities.

Half-page entries
Don't, however, ignore our half-page entries. They are very useful addresses, and all are charming small hotels. You can't have stars on every page.

No fear or favour
Unlike many guides, there is no payment for inclusion. The selection is made *entirely* independently.

Choosing your room
In Venice, you can enormously enhance the quality of your accommodation by securing a good room. Many of the hotels in this guide have rooms which are similar in both price and quality, but others, whilst remaining the same in price, are much more varied in quality. You can quite easily find yourself paying the same rate for a dull box as for a light and airy space with a balcony overlooking a canal, and unless you specifically ask (and make your booking in plenty of time) you are not likely to secure one of the few good rooms. Hoteliers have told us of guests who, on their return visit, ask for the room they had before, not realizing that there are far better ones to be had at the same price. Where appropriate, therefore, we have taken pains to point out which are the rooms you should try for first; in a few cases, we have advised not choosing that hotel at all unless you can secure a particular room. We have not always mentioned room numbers, as these are prone to change.

Hotels, villas, *locande, agriturismo*
The range of accommodation on offer in Venice and North-East Italy should be enough to satisfy all tastes and most pockets, with a variety of names almost as numerous as those describing types of pasta. 'Hotel' is common enough, but so is its Italian equivalent *'albergo'*. *'Villa'* can apply either to a town or country hotel and is used by proprietors with some latitude: occasionally one wonders why a nondescript town house or farmhouse should be called a *villa* while a more elegant building restricts itself to *albergo*. *'Palazzo'* and *'pensione'* generally refer to urban accommodation while *'agriturismo'* means farmhouse bed-and-breakfast, or indeed, self-catering apartments. *'Residence'*, *'relais'*, *'locanda'*, *'castello'* and *'fattoria'* are also found.

The variety that one finds under these various names is extraordinary, from world-ranking luxury hotels to relatively simple guest houses.

Tourist information
The tourist information offices for each province are listed with the relevant maps on pages 15–31. Most cities and a few popular towns also have their own tourist offices offering information on local travel, museums, galleries and festivals.

We list on page 10 Italy's official public holidays when banks and shops are shut and levels of public transport reduced. In North-East Italy, like the rest of the country, each town has its own local holiday, usually the feast day of the patron saint, often celebrated with a fair or fireworks. Venice, of course, stages its annual pre-Lent Carnival and many other events unique to the city, most famous of which are the Biennale, the world's largest contemporary art exhibition which takes place from June to September in odd-numbered years, and the International Film Festival, held on the Lido in early September every year.

New Year's Day (*Capodanno*) Jan 1; Epiphany (*Epifania*) Jan 6; Good Friday (*Venerdì Santo*); Easter Sunday (*Pasqua*); Easter Monday (*Pasquetta*); Liberation Day (*Liberazione*) April 25; May Day (*Festa del Lavoro*) May 1; Assumption of the Virgin (*Ferragosto*) Aug 15; All Saints' Day (*Ognissanti*) Nov 1; Immaculate Conception (*Immacolata Concezione*) Dec 8; Christmas Day (*Natale*) Dec 25; St Stephen's Day (*Santo Stefano*) Dec 26.

Flights
The principal airport for the region is Venice Marco Polo, and there are also small airports at Treviso and Verona which receive limited flights from abroad. Car hire is available at all three.

Pet likes
These are some of the things that stand out for us in many of the hotels in which we stayed. Maybe they will strike you too.

* Wonderful old buildings, sympathetically restored – *palazzi* in Venice, classical villas in the Veneto, castles in the foothills of the Alps, Tyrolean chalets in the mountains
* Hotels in superb positions with glorious views
* Murano glass chandeliers (pretty ones)
* Venetian marble floors (when strewn with rugs)
* Silk damask furnishing fabric (when not overdone)
* 'Buffet' breakfasts with fruit, cheese, cold meats and yogurts
* Spotlessly clean bedrooms and bathrooms – especially high quality in the mountain hotels
* Good quality linen and comfortable pillows

Pet hates
If Venetian hoteliers have a fault, it is that they are happy for their hotels to coast along rather than strive for perfection. This is for the simple reason that they have a captive audience, a constant influx of tourists who keep occupancy rates at a consistently high level. And prices are very high. Stay half an hour away from the city, and you will pay far less for a much larger room. So the hotels which really aim to please, despite their popularity, are the ones which get our highest praise.

* Murano glass chandeliers (hideous ones)
* Venetian marble floors (when coldly bare)
* Silk damask furnishing fabric (when overdone)

Introduction

- 'Continental' breakfasts with inedible cardboard bread
- Hideous minibars
- Inadequate storage space
- Endless white-tiled bathrooms
- Too many bathrooms with shower only, no bathtub

Readers' reports
To all the hundreds of readers who have written with comments on hotels, a sincere 'thank-you'. We attach great importance to your comments and absorb them into the text each year. Please keep writing: for further information see page 32.

How to find an entry
In this guide, the whole-page entries, beginning on page 33, come first, followed by the half-page entries, which begin on page 119.

Hotels in Venice are featured first, subdivided into the city's *sestieri* or districts: San Marco, San Polo, Santa Croce, Castello, Dorsoduro, Cannaregio and the Lagoon Islands, including the Lido. In each subsection of Venice, entries are arranged in alphabetical order by name of hotel.

Hotels outside Venice are grouped according to the province in which they lie: first Veneto (which is the province in which Venice lies), then Lombardia (which accounts for the hotels on the western shores of Lake Garda – we do not explore this province any further as it does not lie in North-East Italy), followed by Friuli-Venezia Giulia, and Trentino-Alto Adige.

Within each of these regional sections, the entries are arranged in alphabetical order by nearest town. If several occur in one town, they are arranged in alphabetical order by name of hotel.

The half-page entries follow the same pattern: Venice, subdivided into its *sestieri*, followed by Veneto, Lombardia, Friuli-Venezia Giulia and Trentino-Alto Adige.

To find a hotel in a particular area, use the maps following this introduction to locate the appropriate pages.

To locate a specific hotel, whose name you know, or a hotel in a place you know, use the indexes at the back, which list entries both by name and by nearest place name.

How to read an entry
At the top of each entry is a coloured bar highlighting the name of the town or village, or in the case of Venice, district, where the establishment is located, along with a categorization which gives some clue to its character. These categories are, as far as possible, self-explanatory.

Fact boxes
The fact box given for each hotel follows a standard pattern; the explanation that follows is for full- and half-page entries.

Tel and Fax The number in brackets is the area code from within Italy. If you are calling from abroad, you will need to drop the zero after the international code for Italy (39).

Location The location and setting of the hotel are briefly described; car parking facilities follow, except in Venice. In cities such as Padua and Verona, few hotels have their own car parking – most depend on arrangements with nearby garages. The prices are set by the garages and not by the hotels, so please check first.

In Venice hotels, under **vaporetto**, we tell you where the nearest *vaporetto* or water-bus landing stage is; we also indicate if the hotel has a water door on to a canal, so that you can arrive by gondola or water taxi. For those arriving by foot from the nearest *vaporetto* stop, lugging the luggage through the narrow streets and over the numerous little bridges that span the canals can be exhausting, especially if the hotel is none too close. If you prefer, you can enlist a porter to transport your bags, although they are very expensive. Porters are often available at San Marco and Rialto, but if you are arriving at any other landing stage, it is best to call your hotel and arrange for a porter to meet you.

Meals Under this heading we list the meals available. For breakfast, you may find either a continental breakfast or a self-service buffet breakfast (increasingly common) or both. We do not state whether a hotel provides room service, as this can vary from the provision of a cup of tea to full meals and 24-hour service. Generally, only the luxury hotels provide full room service, while small, smart ones might provide a limited service, and humble ones none at all; if in doubt, check with the hotel.

Prices In this guide, we have given room and meal prices in lire, rather than using price bands as in many of the other guides in the series. One reason for this is that in Venice there is such a large choice of hotels within such a small area that a fix on cost is an essential aid to making a choice of hotel.

The basic prices are per room, and first we give the range, from the cheapest single to the most expensive room in the hotel, be it a double, triple, family room or suite. Where hotels have different tariffs for low and high season, our range is from the cheapest room at the low season rate to the most expensive at the high season rate. The vast majority of hotels in this guide have both low and high season rates; many have a mid-season rate in between. It's often difficult to know when is low and when is high season (Carnival time in February is classed as high season) and in practice some hoteliers will charge according to how full their hotel is when you want to stay. Because of this confusing price range, we also give the price of a standard double room (both low and high season rates) so that you can see at a glance what you might be expected to pay. If the room price includes breakfast (which it generally does) we say so; otherwise we give the price of breakfast separately. This generally refers to a continental breakfast, although it may be buffet style. Many hotels will include a continental or light buffet breakfast in the price and offer other dishes at extra cost.

Where hotels offer dinner, we have indicated the lowest price per person you might expect to pay for a three-course meal without wine.

Unless half board is obligatory in a hotel, we have not mentioned its cost. If you are interested in half-board, ask the hotel for prices. Where half-board is obligatory, we have quoted prices per person in lire.

Check the price first. To avoid unpleasant surprises, always double-check the price at the time of booking. Sometimes prices go up after we have been to press, sometimes there is a seasonal or other variation from the printed version.

Rooms Under this heading we indicate the number and type – single, double, triple, family and suites – and whether the rooms have baths (usually with shower or shower attachment as well) or just showers. Unless stated you can assume that the bath or shower room will include a WC and washbasin. If you particularly want a bathtub (*bagno*) in your bathroom rather than just a shower, you should make this clear when you book, in case the receptionist thinks you simply mean you want a room with a bathroom.

If you have a large number of people to accommodate, do ask the hotel if rooms can be arranged to suit you. Although hotels may have one or two suites, rooms are generally not large, but sometimes connecting rooms are available. Very often the hotel will be able to supply a third bed in a double or twin room for a supplement.

Of the facilities we list in the rooms, in most cases the telephones will be direct-dial. In the most recently renovated hotels you may also find a fax/modem point. Many hotels now have cable or satellite TV in addition to the normal terrestrial channels: check with the hotel as to which, if any, foreign channels are available. We have not listed central heating as a facility, as all the hotels in the book have this; we do, however, indicate when a hotel has air-conditioning. Most hotels in the guide do, although in a few cases, this may mean bulky free-standing units.

Facilities Under facilities we list: public rooms; lift; courtyard, garden or terrace; indoor or outdoor swimming pool; tennis court; fitness and sauna facilities.

Credit cards We use the following abbreviations:
  AE   American Express
  DC   Diners Club

MC   MasterCard (Access/Eurocard)
V   Visa (Barclaycard/Bank Americard/Carte Bleue etc)

Children Children are nearly always welcome in Italian hotels (and restaurants), and many hotels offer discounts on third beds for children sharing their parents' room. Some hotels clearly wish to offer their guests plenty of peace and quiet, and therefore discourage too many mini-guests. Many Venice hotels, being small and delicately furnished, are not necessarily suited to young children; the breakfast rooms in particular, with their small tables and chairs, can present a problem. Where we have written that children are 'welcome' rather than 'accepted', we indicate that the hotel's proprietor was particularly enthused by the prospect of young guests, and may well have special facilities.

Disabled Venice hotels are not the most suitable for those in wheelchairs, and many of the hotels in this guide are without lifts or special facilities. Where facilities exist, they are indicated.

Pets 'Accepted' means that the hotel is happy to accommodate well-behaved small animals. Sometimes they stipulate that animals are not allowed in public rooms. A small daily fee may be charged.

Closed Venice hotels rarely close. A handful shut down for a short period in winter. The same goes for hotels on the Veneto Plain. Hotels around Lake Garda, however, and in the mountains, are much more prone to periods of closure. Dates vary considerably, but as a rule, Lake Garda hotels close during the winter, while mountain hotels are open for the skiing season and high summer, but may close for a period in spring or early summer and again in autumn/early winter. The dates we give under the heading 'Closed' are those supplied to us by the hotel.

The final entry in a fact box is the name of the **Proprietor**(s). Where a hotel is run by a manager, we give his or her name.

Hotel location maps

North-Eastern Italy

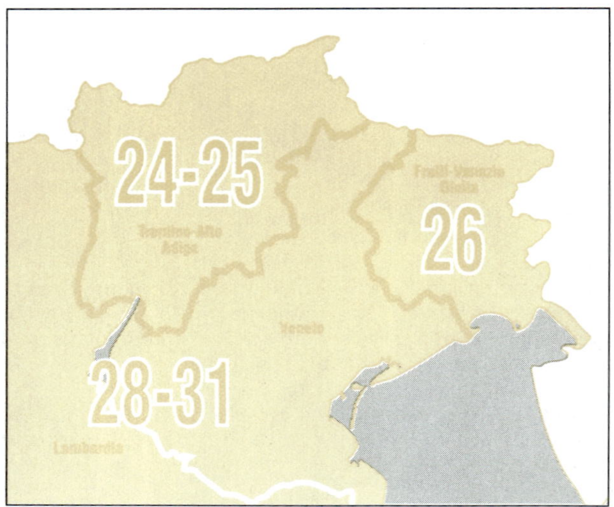

Venice and its Lagoon

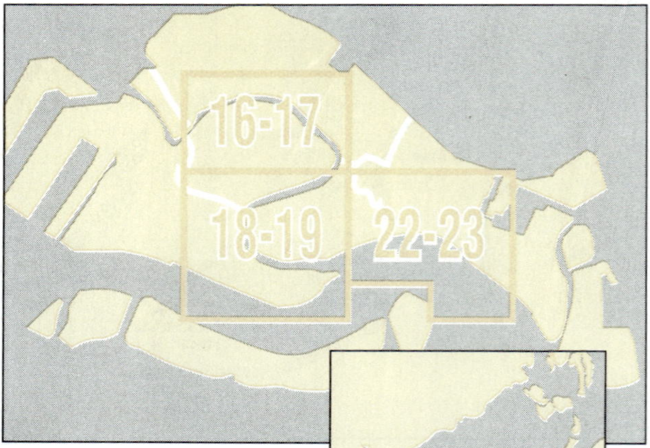

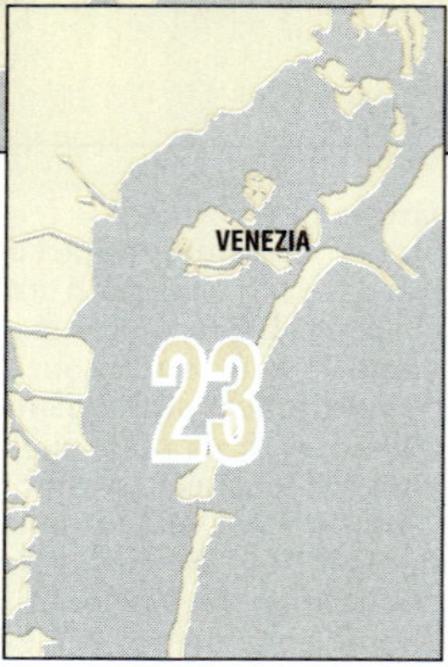

Tourist information
Azienda di Promozione
Turistica di Venezia
Castello 4421
Venezia
Tel (041) 5298701

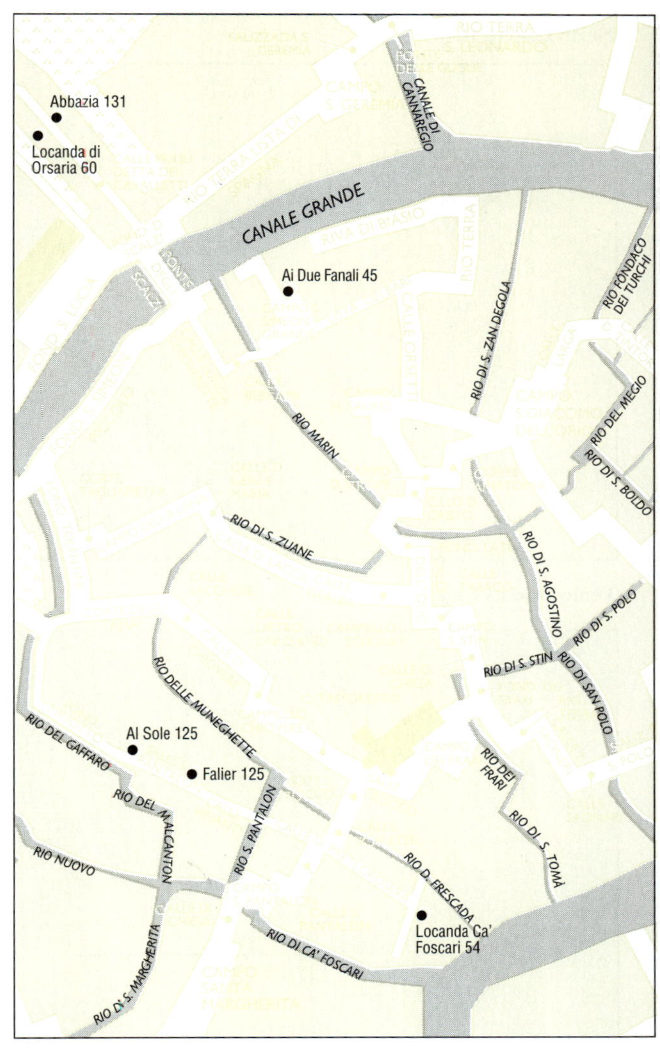

Cannaregio

Very much a residential area, full of charm and character, Cannaregio is bounded to the north by the Lagoon (Fondamente Nuove is the main starting point for *vaporetti* to the islands), and to the south by a long sweep of the Grand Canal. Most prized of the many lovely *palazzi* along here is the Ca' d'Oro, with its pink, sugar-spun Venetian Gothic façade. The bulk of tourists are drawn to Lista di Spagna and Strada Nova, two sections of the route from the station to the Rialto, leaving the rest of the district delightfully quiet at all times of the year. Don't miss the Ghetto, the world's oldest, nor the wonderfully over-the-top interior of Gesuiti, near Fondamente Nuove.

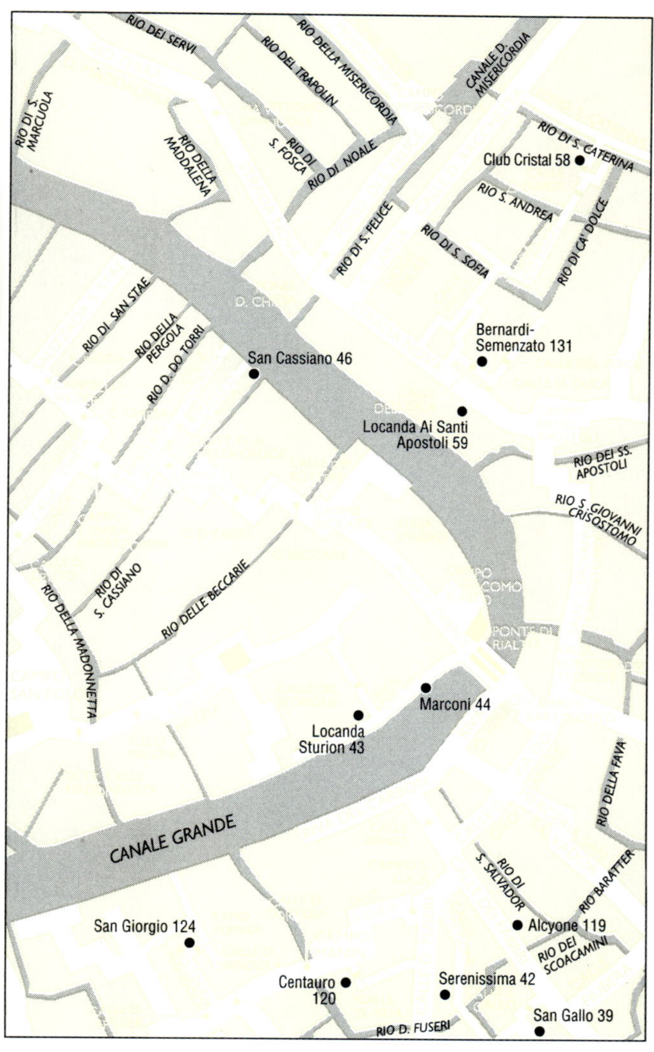

San Polo and Santa Croce

The *sestiere* of San Polo is lively and full of little shops, restaurants and bars, and of course, the colourful Rialto markets. Trading began here in the 11thC, and ever since, the *erberia* and *pescheria* markets have flourished. For just as long, the Rialto Bridge has attracted people; today it swarms with tourists, and the canal below is equally thick with river traffic. Built in 1588, it marks the centre of the city. Also in San Polo is the great Frari church, and Tintoretto's remarkable cycle of paintings in the Scuola di San Rocco. Santa Croce is mainly a humble area, with the vast car park, Piazzale Roma, as well as a stretch of *palazzi* along the Grand Canal, including one of our hotels.

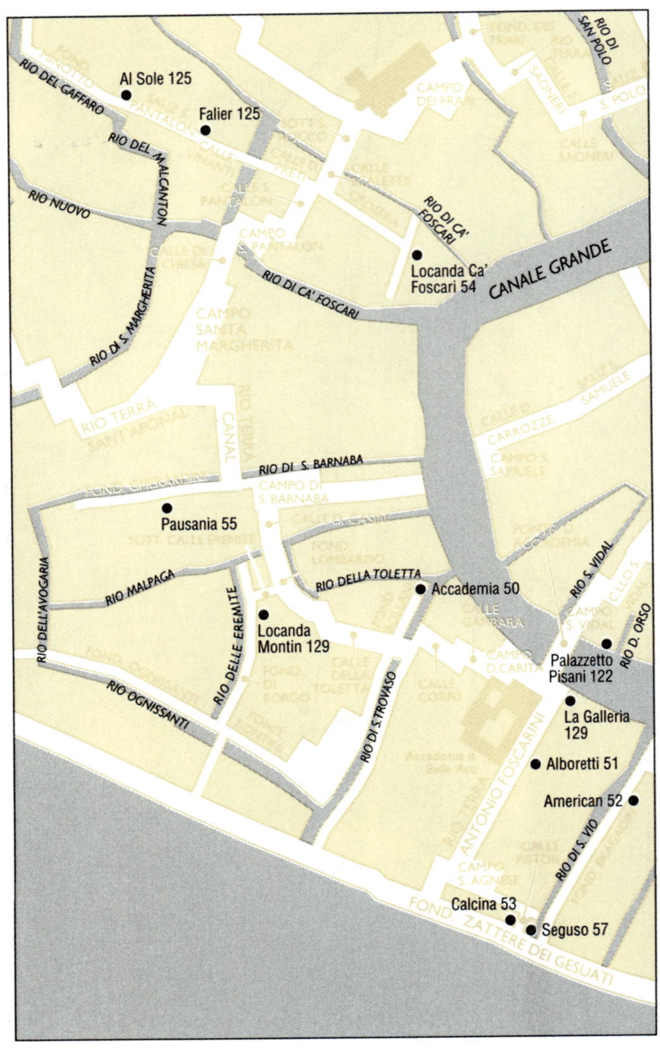

Dorsoduro

Only in 1854 was a second bridge constructed to cross the Grand Canal; in 1932 it was replaced with a temporary wooden structure, but, much loved, it has remained in place to this day as the Accademia Bridge which links the *sestieri* of San Marco and Dorsoduro. Bordered on one side by the Grand Canal, on the other by the wide Giudecca Canal, and criss-crossed by tributaries, Dorsoduro is tranquil and picturesque, yet close to the main sights. Its chief attractions are the Accademia Gallery and the Peggy Guggenheim Collection, as well as the churches of Santa Maria della Salute and Gesuati. Dig deeper and you will find the lovely and very old church of San Nicolò dei Mendicoli,

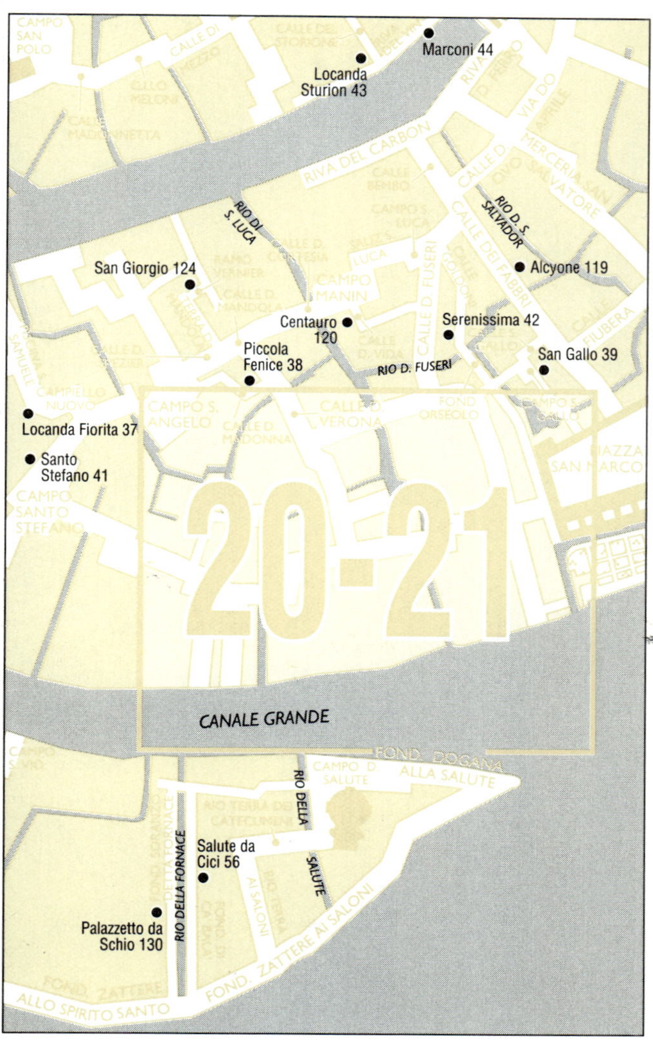

the gondola boatyard, and charming little spaces such as Campiello Barbaro and Campo San Barnaba. One of the greatest pleasures of Dorsoduro is to linger at a pavement café along the sun-soaked Zattere.

San Marco

Piazza San Marco is the heart of Venice, a fitting space from which to admire the great Basilica and Doge's Palace. Napoleon called it the 'most elegant drawing room in Europe' and on a balmy summer's night when the café orchestras are playing and the swirling daytime crowds have dwindled, his description is still apt. On one side of the Piazza is the Lagoon; on the other, ▶

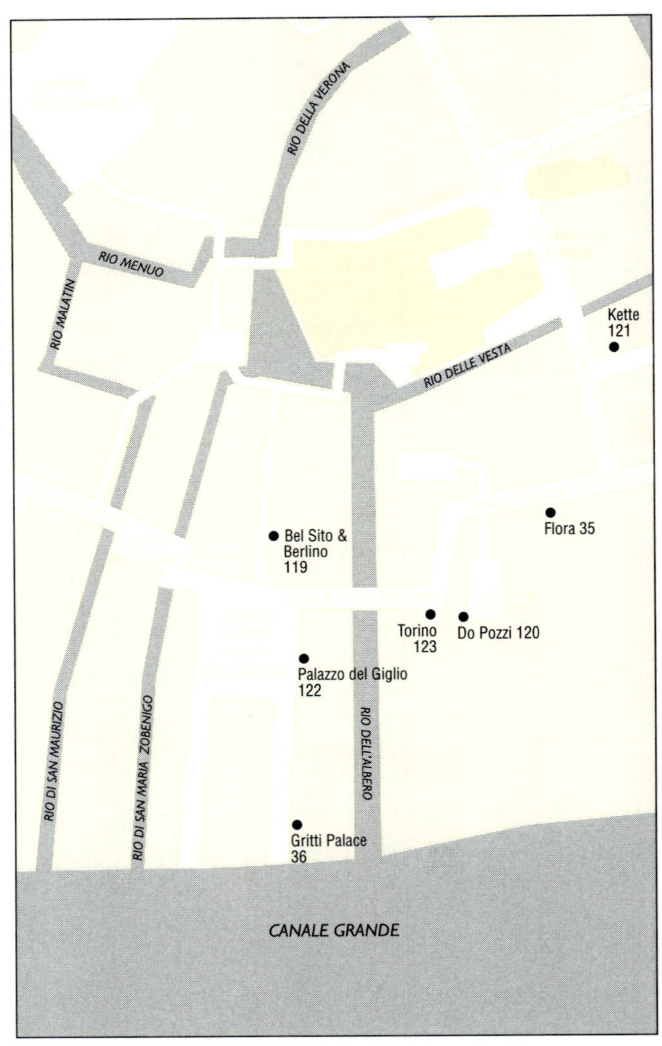

narrow streets full of shops, both for tourists and locals, fan out over the network of canals. In this district you will also find the opera house, Teatro La Fenice – or what's left of it – the spacious Campo Santo Stefano and the charming Bovolo staircase, tucked away in a quiet corner. You will also find the greatest concentration of charming small hotels.

Hotel location maps

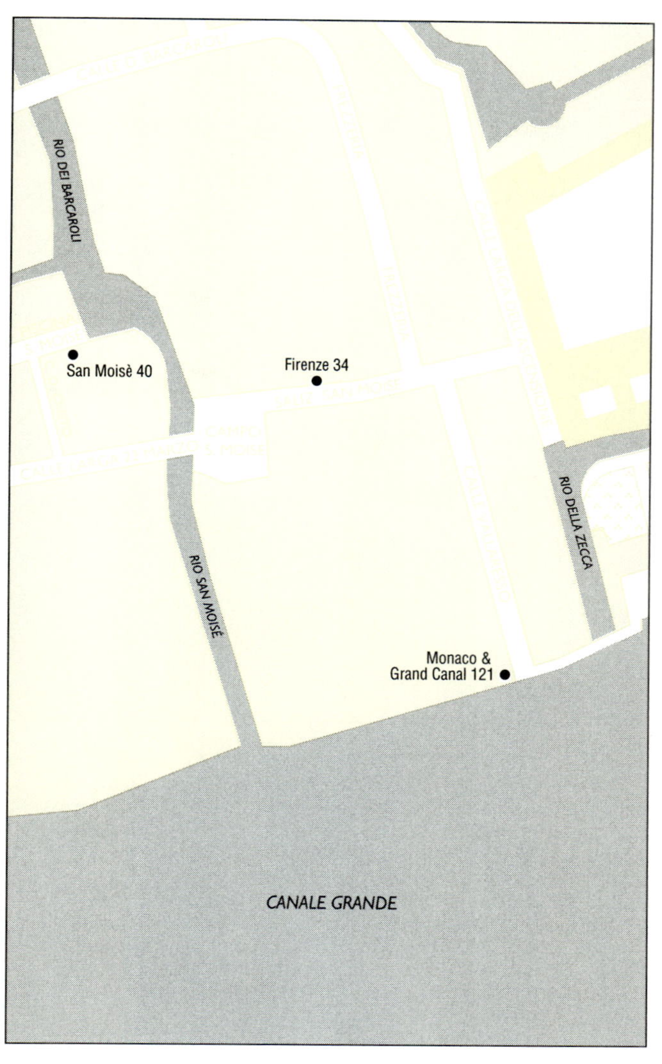

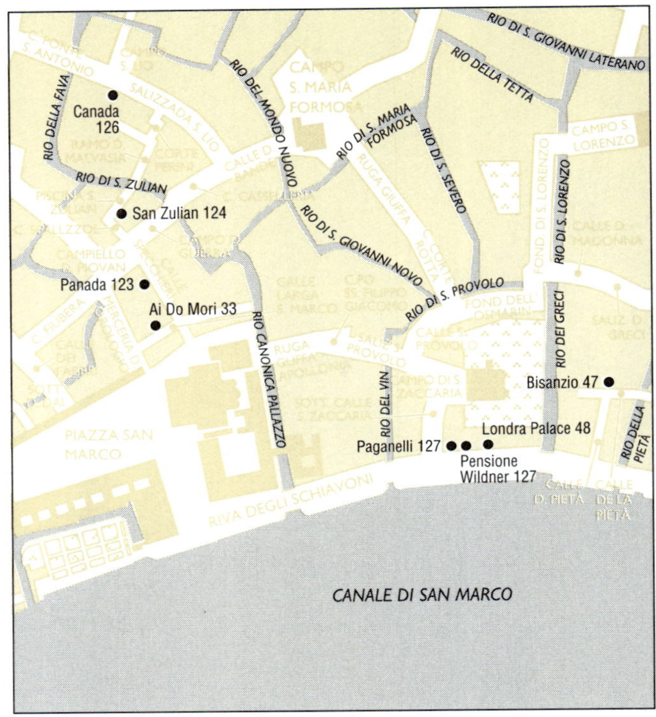

Castello

A marvellously varied district, Castello includes the mighty Riva degli Schiavoni, whose many hotels enjoy unrivalled views across the Lagoon to the island of San Giorgio Maggiore, with its landmark church of the same name by Palladio. Behind the waterfront lies a different Venice: quiet, dusty squares, pretty canals and lovely paintings – principally in San Giovanni in Bragora, Santa Maria Formosa, San Zaccaria, Scuola di San Giorgio degli Schiavoni, Fondazione Querini Stampalia and Santi Giovanni e Paolo. To the west is Arsenale, from where sprang the city's great maritime prowess.

Venetian Lagoon Islands

No visit to Venice is complete without a trip to at least some of the islands in the magical, mysterious Lagoon. Many centuries ago the people of the mainland were forced by invaders to seek refuge amongst the sandbanks; they built protective walls and thriving communities grew up, now long since disappeared. Murano has been a centre of glass-blowing since medieval times; San Michele is the cemetery island, and includes the tombs of famous artists and writers; Burano is packed with gaily painted houses; Torcello is the enigmatic cradle of the Venetian civilization, with only two beautiful churches to remind us of its days of supremacy; the Lido, developed in the 19thC is both city suburb and seaside resort, and retains the faintly melancholy air of the once-fashionable. Its great hotels are filled with conventions, but

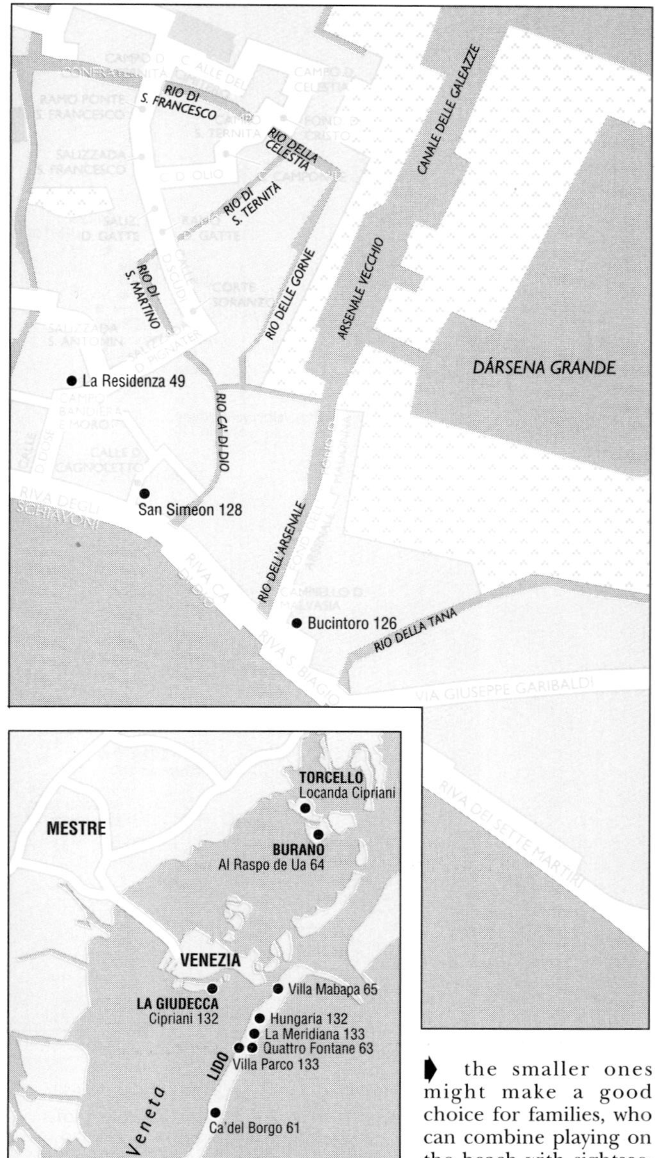

the smaller ones might make a good choice for families, who can combine playing on the beach with sightseeing in Venice.

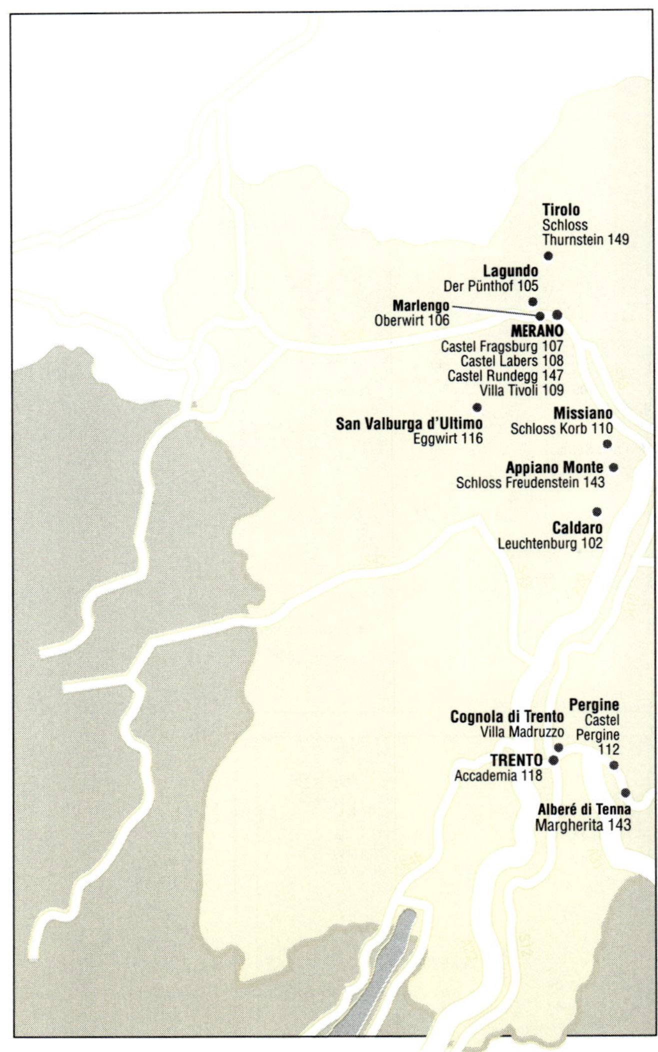

Trentino-Alto Adige

The province of Trentino-Alto Adige is a world away from Venice and its great plain. It feels like Austria, has a special autonomous statute and is largely German-speaking. Owners and staff of the Alpine hotels you will find in its mountains may not even speak Italian ... you are more likely to be greeted in German, and they may speak English. Place names are extremely confusing, as each town and village, mountain and valley has both an Italian and German name. We have given the Italian translation, occasionally referring to the German as well. Hotels are often Tyrolean chalets, with wooden furniture, ceramic stoves, traditional fabrics; the food too, is mainly Austrian: dumplings, ▶

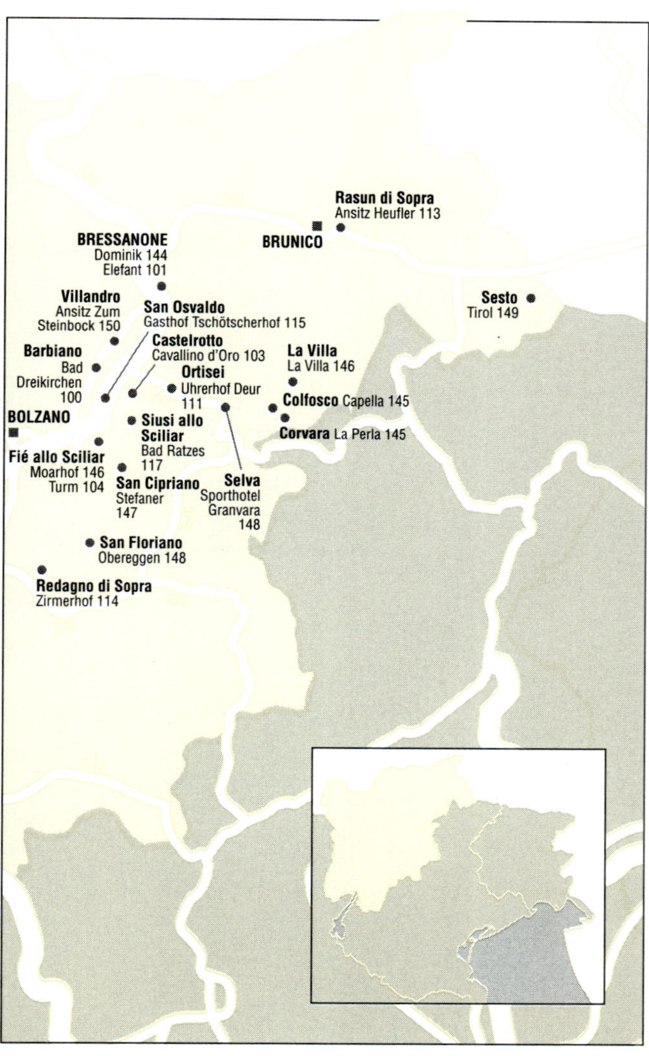

goulash and *sauerkraut* feature on the simpler menus, while the more sophisticated hotels serve creative variations on the theme. The scenery amongst the Dolomites is breathtakingly beautiful, and there are plenty of activities to pursue both in winter and summer.

Tourist information

Piazza Walther 8	132 Corso 111	9 Viale Stazione
Bolzano 39100	Novembre	Bressanone
Trentino-Alto Adige	Trento	Tel (0472) 836401
Tel (0471) 970660	Tel (0461) 980000	

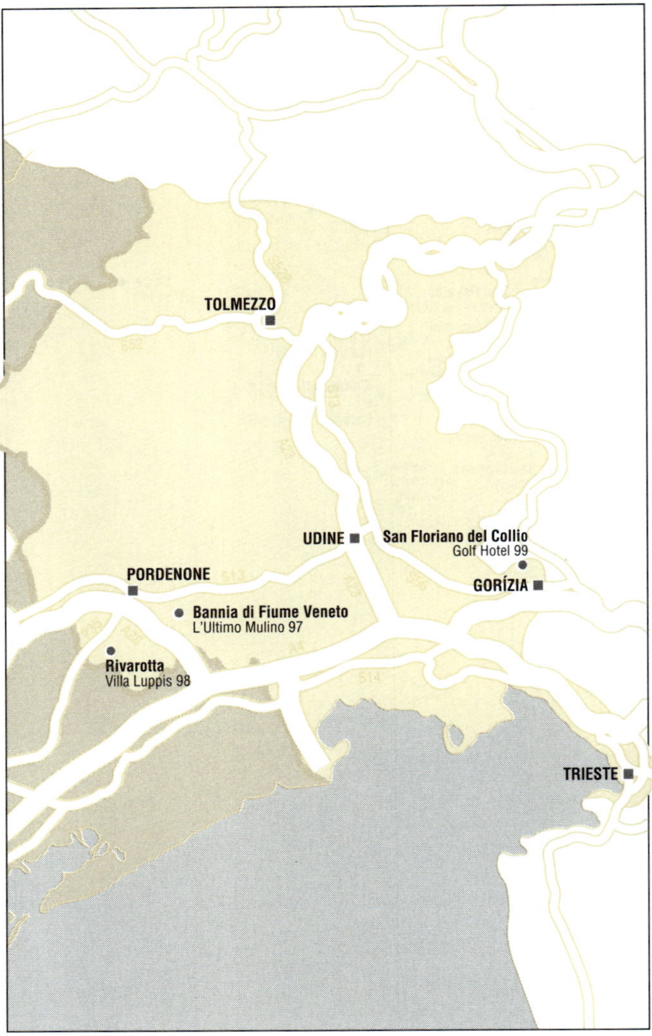

TOLMEZZO
UDINE
San Floriano del Collio
Golf Hotel 99
PORDENONE
GORÍZIA
Bannia di Fiume Veneto
L'Ultimo Mulino 97
Rivarotta
Villa Luppis 98
TRIESTE

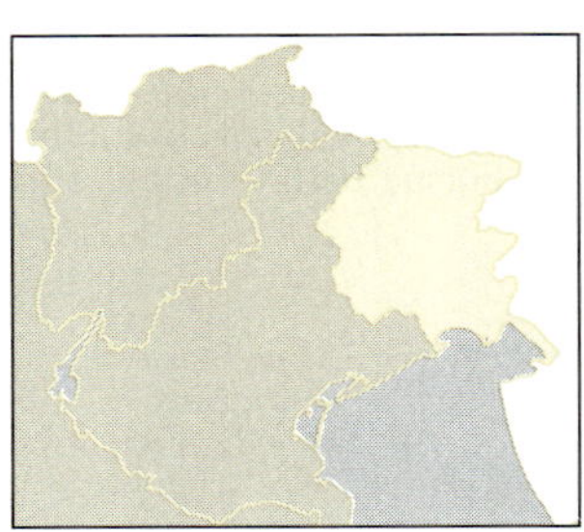

Friuli-Venezia Giulia
The province accounts for the eastern part of the Veneto Plain as it curves towards the border with Slovenia. To the north and the border with Austria it rises to the Carnic Alps with its alpine meadows and pine forests. Some 20 years ago the area was devastated by an earthquake. Some of the most beautiful and verdant scenery in all Italy can be found in this corner of the country, and yet it is hardly visited, and hotels are thin on the ground. There are some old-fashioned hostelries in Tolmezzo and the beautifully situated spa town of Arta Terme. The main cities are Trieste, with its air of faded grandeur, and Udine, a busy industrial town with a lovely old *piazza* and cathedral. Our small selection of hotels can be found mainly in the west of the province.

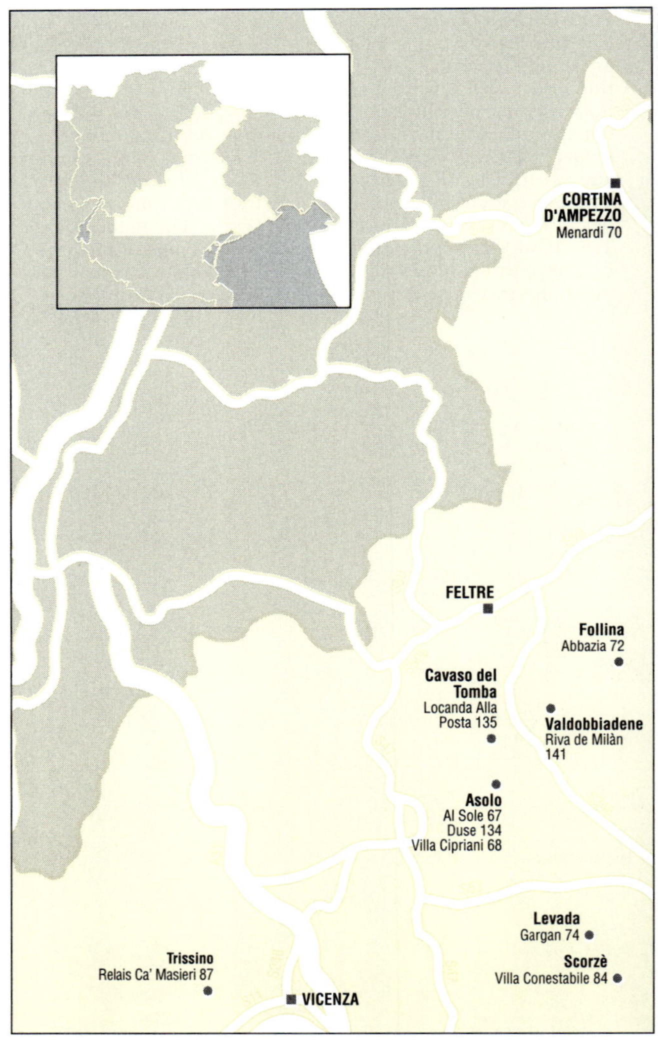

Veneto

The province of Veneto accounts for much of the great Veneto Plain, but to its north it thrusts through the mountains to reach the Austrian border. The bulk of our hotels are on the plain, in both countryside and in the plain's great cities, Vicenza, Padua and Treviso. If you want to stay within easy reach of Venice, there are plenty of choices. To the north of the province, where the foothills of the Dolomites begin to rise from the flat landscape, you will find some delightful places; the charming hilltop village of Asolo is particularly well served. To the west, there are choices in the vibrant and lovely city of Verona, in the fertile wine-country around it, and along the eastern shores of Lake Garda.

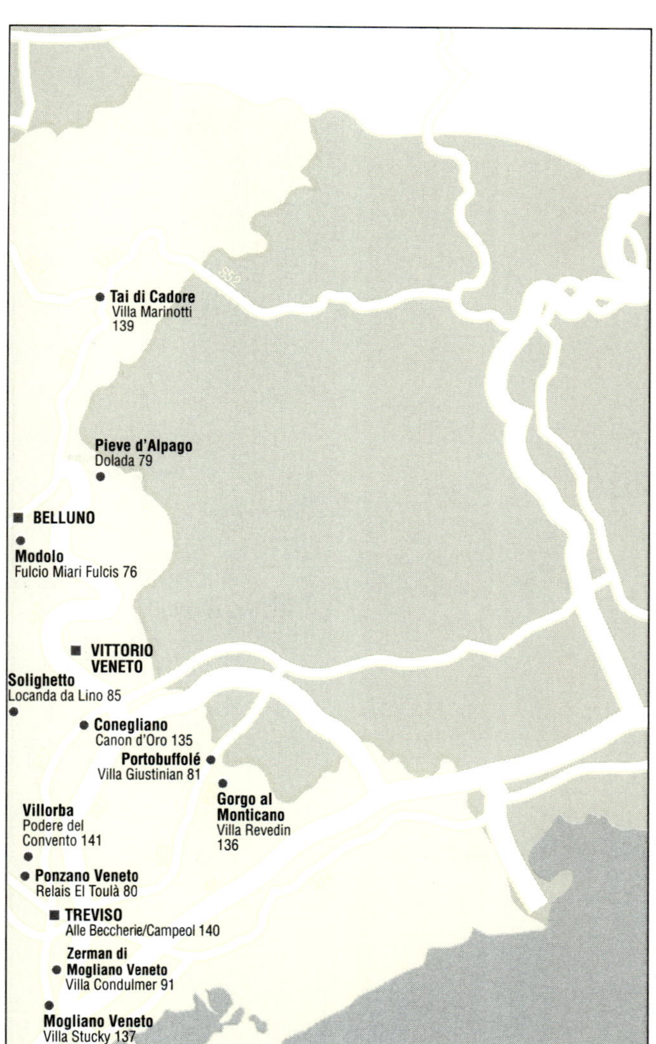
Tai di Cadore
Villa Marinotti
139
Pieve d'Alpago
Dolada 79
BELLUNO
Modolo
Fulcio Miari Fulcis 76
VITTORIO VENETO
Solighetto
Locanda da Lino 85
Conegliano
Canon d'Oro 135
Portobuffolé
Villa Giustinian 81
Villorba
Podere del
Convento 141
Gorgo al Monticano
Villa Revedin
136
Ponzano Veneto
Relais El Toulà 80
TREVISO
Alle Beccherie/Campeol 140
Zerman di
Mogliano Veneto
Villa Condulmer 91
Mogliano Veneto
Villa Stucky 137

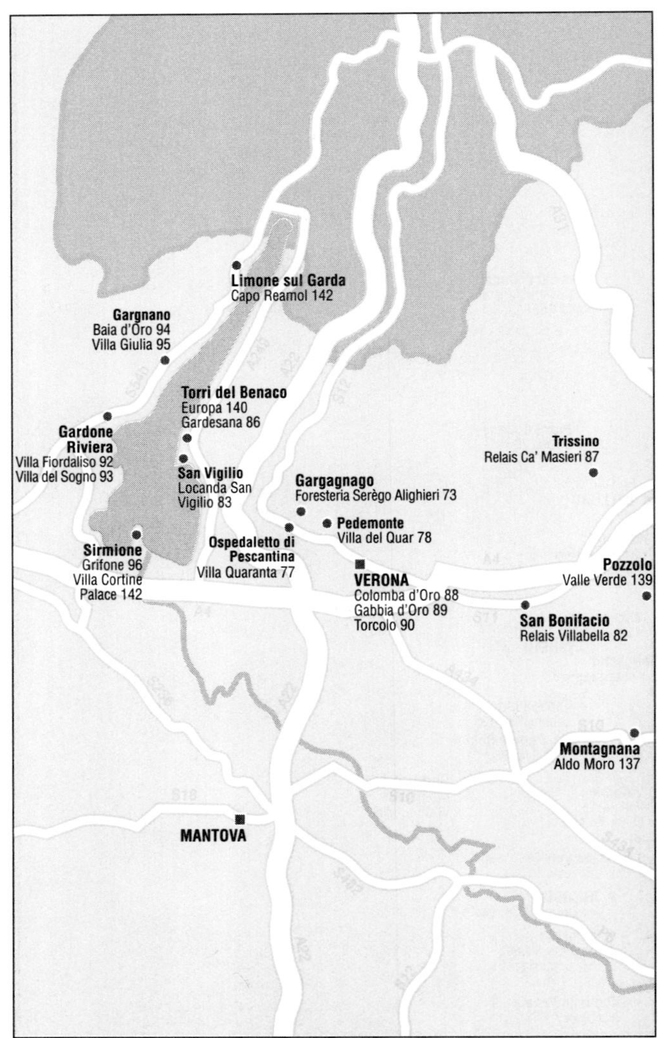

Lombardia

The only part of the province of Lombardia that concerns this guide is the area on the western shores of Lake Garda, the largest lake in Italy. It makes an ideal summertime playground, where you can windsurf, sail or cruise the lake by ferry. With a backdrop of snow-capped mountains, the shores are strung along with pretty villages, little harbours and waterfront promenades. To the south, the Sirmione Peninsula points into the lake, and the old town of Sirmione is the most picturesque of all.

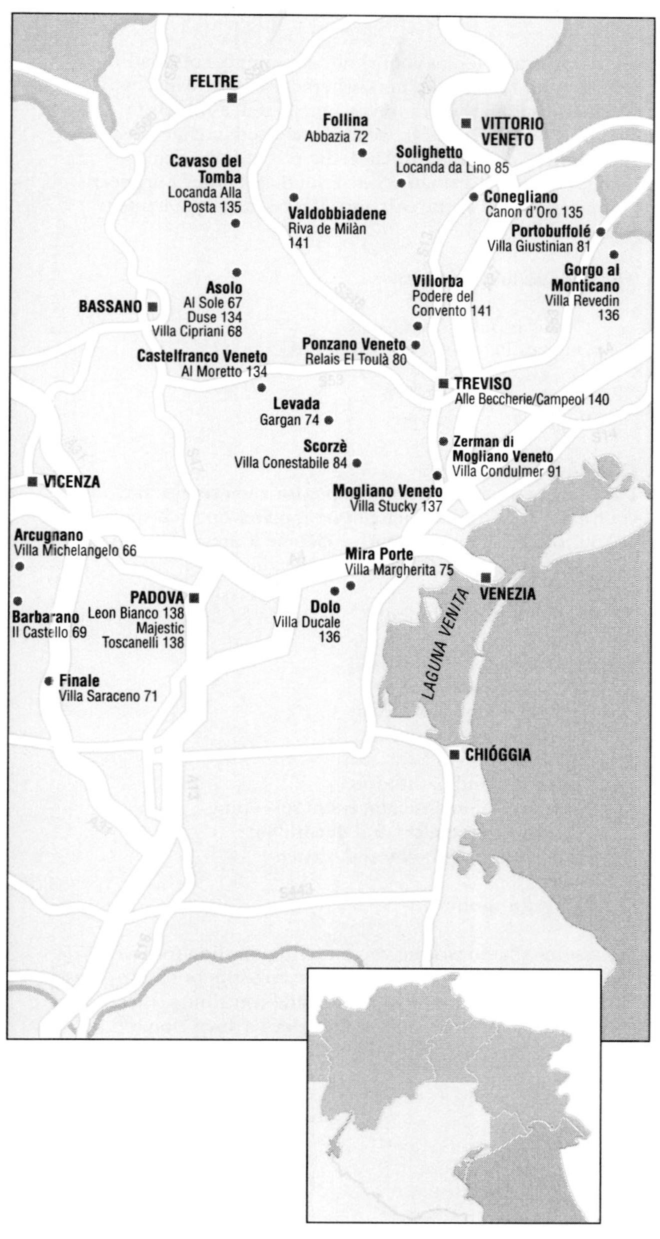

FELTRE
Follina
Abbazia 72
VITTORIO VENETO
Cavaso del Tomba
Locanda Alla Posta 135
Solighetto
Locanda da Lino 85
Conegliano
Canon d'Oro 135
Valdobbiadene
Riva de Milàn 141
Portobuffolé
Villa Giustinian 81
Gorgo al Monticano
Villa Revedin 136
Asolo
Al Sole 67
Duse 134
Villa Cipriani 68
BASSANO
Villorba
Podere del Convento 141
Castelfranco Veneto
Al Moretto 134
Ponzano Veneto
Relais El Toulà 80
TREVISO
Alle Beccherie/Campeol 140
Levada
Gargan 74
Scorzè
Villa Conestabile 84
Zerman di Mogliano Veneto
Villa Condulmer 91
VICENZA
Mogliano Veneto
Villa Stucky 137
Arcugnano
Villa Michelangelo 66
Mira Porte
Villa Margherita 75
VENEZIA
PADOVA
Leon Bianco 138
Majestic
Toscanelli 138
Dolo
Villa Ducale 136
Barbarano
Il Castello 69
LAGUNA VENITA
Finale
Villa Saraceno 71
CHIÓGGIA

Please write and tell us about your experiences of small hotels, guest houses and inns, whether good or bad, whether listed in this edition or not. As well as hotels in Venice & North-East Italy, we are interested in charming small hotels in: Britain, Ireland, the rest of Italy, France, Spain, Portugal, Germany, Switzerland and other European countries, as well as the east and west coasts of the United States.

The address to write to is:

Charming Small Hotel Guides,
Duncan Petersen Publishing Ltd,
31 Ceylon Road,
London, W14 OPY
England.

Checklist
Please use a separate sheet of paper for each report; include your name, address and telephone number on each sheet.
   Your reports are particularly welcome if they are typed and organized under the following headings:

Name of establishment
Town or village
Full address and postcode
Telephone number
Time and duration of visit
The building and setting
Public rooms
Bedrooms and bathrooms
Standards of maintenance, housekeeping
Standards of comfort and decoration
Atmosphere, welcome and service
Food
Value for money

We assume that in writing you have no objection to your views being published unpaid, either verbatim or in an edited version. Names of major outside contributors are acknowledged in the guide, at the editor's discretion.

San Marco

Town guest-house

Ai Do Mori

We had great difficulty finding the Ai Do Mori – reception is on the first floor and only a lantern discreetly displays the name on the street. We arrived to find the vivacious young owner divulging tips to some guests: "Don't take a gondola on the Grand Canal. A *vaporetto* is much cheaper. Take a gondola on the little canals and see a different Venice."

At the time of our visit there were no facilities for serving breakfast and only half the bedrooms had bathrooms, but Antonella Bernardi is constantly making changes and plans to add a breakfast room and bathrooms shortly. We suspect that in a year or so it will be upgraded from its one-star status.

The modest white-walled bedrooms are spacious and light. Nos 6 and 7 have rustic beams, but by far the most desirable is the one Antonella endearingly calls "the painter room". Up a steep staircase, tucked under the eaves, it is small – just accommodating the double bed and a few carefully chosen pieces of furniture – but has a small suntrap of a roof terrace, from where you can almost reach out and touch the figures on the Basilica San Marco; and this for just L150,000 a night.
Nearby Piazza San Marco; San Zulian.

Calle Larga San Marco, San Marco 658, 30124 Venezia
Tel (041) 5204817/5289293
Fax (041) 5205328
Location near junction with Calle Spadaria, just N of Piazzetta dei Leoni; **vaporetto** San Marco
Meals none
Prices rooms L95,000–L275,000; standard double L150,000 (10% discount in low season)
Rooms 11; 10 double and twin, triple and family, 4 with bath, 2 with shower, 4 with washbasin; 1 single with washbasin; all rooms have phone, TV, air-conditioning, hairdrier, safe
Credit cards MC, V
Children accepted
Disabled not suitable
Pets not accepted
Closed 3 weeks in Jan
Proprietor Antonella Bernardi

San Marco

Firenze

The distinguishing features of the Firenze are its rooftop terrace
– reached from the top floor by an external staircase – where you
can breakfast in summer whilst picking out the landmarks, and
the three bedrooms with private terrace which cost no more
than ones without.

The building, just along from the florid, blackened façade of
San Moisè, has a fine marble-and-iron art nouveau front (in need
of restoration – the owner has plans); at the turn of the century
it was an Austrian hat factory, as the splendid first floor windows
announce. Inside, a recent total renovation has left the bedrooms uniform: unadorned Venetian marble floors (not cosy),
peach-coloured walls, pale green headboards and matching cupboards, pretty Murano glass wall lights and white ruched net curtains. The first-floor breakfast room was designed to echo the
famous café Florian in Piazza San Marco, with polished wood
benches and tables lining the walls, but it doesn't quite come off
and feels merely awkward. Choose the Firenze – managed with
good humour by its owner, Signor Fabris – during the summer
when you can make use of the terrace.
Nearby Piazza San Marco.

Salizzada San Moisè, San Marco
1490, 30124 Venezia
Tel (041) 5222858
Fax (041) 5202668
Location 30 m from Piazza San
Marco, alongside San Moisè;
vaporetto San Marco
Meals breakfast
Prices rooms L100,000–
L340,000; standard double
L140,000–L340,000; breakfast
included
Rooms 25; 22 double, 3 single,
all with bath; all rooms have
phone, TV, air-conditioning,
minibar, hairdrier, safe
Facilities breakfast room,
rooftop terrace, lift
Credit cards AE, MC, V
Children accepted
Disabled not suitable
Pets accepted
Closed never
Proprietor Paolo Fabris

San Marco

Flora

Such is the popularity of this small hotel, tucked away down a cul-de-sac close to San Marco, that to get a room here you have to book weeks, even months in advance. You only need to glimpse the garden to know why it is sought after. Creepers, fountains and flowering shrubs cascading from stone urns create an enchanting setting for breakfast, tea or an evening drink in summer.

The lobby is small and inviting, enhanced by the views of the garden through a glass arch; the atmosphere is one of friendly efficiency. There are some charming double bedrooms with painted carved antiques and other typically Venetian furnishings, but beware of other comparatively spartan rooms, some of which are barely big enough for one, let alone two. Coveted rooms include two on the ground floor facing the garden and the three spacious corner rooms, the topmost of which has a marvellous view of Santa Maria della Salute. These rooms represent value for money; others do not. The venerable Flora has been run by the charming Romanelli family, father, son and grandson, for the past 35 years.

Nearby Piazza San Marco.

Calle Larga XXII Marzo, San Marco 2283/a, 30124 Venezia
Tel (041) 5205844
Fax (041) 5228217
Location 300 m from Piazza San Marco in cul-de-sac off Calle Larga XXII Marzo; **vaporetto** San Marco
Meals breakfast
Prices rooms L190,000–L315,000; standard double L260,000–L315,000; breakfast included
Rooms 44; 32 double and twin, 6 single, 6 family, all with bath or shower; all rooms have phone, TV, air-conditioning, hairdrier, safe
Facilities reading room, breakfast room, bar, lift, garden
Credit cards AE, DC, MC, V
Children accepted
Disabled two rooms on ground floor
Pets accepted
Closed never
Proprietors Roger and Joel Romanelli

San Marco

Gritti Palace

Of the three great hotels in Venice – the Danieli, the Cipriani and the Gritti – this is our favourite, and the one which most closely reflects the spirit of this incomparably beautiful city. The Danieli is far too large for us to include, but at under 100 rooms apiece, we have allowed ourselves the liberty of including the other two: they are individual and intimate, and anyway no hotel guide to Venice would be complete without them.

All the bedrooms at the Gritti, the 15thC *palazzo* of Doge Andrea Gritti which opened as a hotel in 1948, are stunning; at least all the ones we saw were – tell us if you disagree. Of the eight exquisite Canal Views suites, our favourite was the Hemingway, in restful shades of pale green. Service is immaculate, the atmosphere patrician yet friendly, and the prices, whilst lofty, far more reasonable than the Cipriani's. And, as Somerset Maugham pointed out, there are few greater pleasures in life than taking a drink on the terrace at sunset, watching the Salute opposite bathed in lovely colour. Before bed, he advises, glance at the portrait of old Andrea Gritti, who, after a tumultuous life, lived his last years here in peace.

Nearby Teatro La Fenice; Piazza San Marco; Accademia.

Campo Santa Maria del Giglio, San Marco 2467, 30124 Venezia
Tel (041) 794611
Fax (041) 5200942
Location in *campo* on Grand Canal; **vaporetto** Santa Maria del Giglio or by water taxi
Meals breakfast, lunch, dinner
Prices rooms L460,000–L3,400,000; standard double L780,000; breakfast L33,000–L55,000
Rooms 93; 80 double and twin, 7 single, 6 suites, all with bath; all rooms have phone, TV, fax/modem point, air-conditioning, minibar, hairdrier
Facilities sitting room, dining room, bar, meeting room, lift, terrace
Credit cards AE, DC, MC, V
Children accepted
Disabled no special facilities, but access possible
Pets accepted
Closed never
Manager Massimo Feriani

San Marco

Town guest-house

Locanda Fiorita

If you are looking for rock-bottom prices and a quiet yet central location, look no further than this bargain one star, a red-painted villa tucked away in a quiet, little-visited square off Campo Santo Stefano. Rooms are small and functional, with modern white furniture which include desks, bedside tables, even beds. Our reporter found her bed surprisingly comfortable, but noted the skimpy towels and lack of shelves, though there was plenty of cupboard space in her room. 'With its beamed ceiling, mint-coloured walls and large windows it was a perfectly pleasant room in which to wake up,' she comments, 'especially when one reflects on what it cost'. No. 10 is the 'honeymoon room', with cupids painted on the wall and a tiny, rather public terrace. Breakfast is taken either at tiny triangular tables set along the wall in the reception area, or, more comfortably, in your room. In summer, the terrace which runs along the front of the building is covered in a pergola of vines, and there are colourful flowers in window boxes. The new owners are planning improvements, and to open up an annexe next door. More reports please.
Nearby Piazza San Marco; Accademia gallery.

Campiello Nuovo, Santo Stefano, San Marco 3457, 30124 Venezia
Tel (041) 5234754
Fax (041) 5228043
Location a little square off Campo Santo Stefano/Calle dei Frati; **vaporetto** San Samuele
Meals breakfast
Prices rooms L80,000–L140,000; standard double L140,000
Rooms 10; 8 double, 2 single, 9 with shower and WC, 1 without; all rooms have phone, fan, hairdrier; 5 have TV
Facilities reception/breakfast area, small terrace
Credit cards AE, MC, V
Children accepted
Disabled access difficult
Pets accepted
Closed never
Proprietor Renato Colombera

San Marco

Piccola Fenice

Perhaps by the time you read this, the Teatro La Fenice will have begun to rise from the ashes, but on our visit it was still a stark shell. The famous adjacent hotel, Fenice et des Artistes, where performers used to put up, was looking too gloomy and faded for us to include, but we were impressed by its new sister hotel, the Piccola Fenice. This consists of seven suites sleeping between two and six people, all with large rooms, including bathrooms tiled in pretty colours, with generous basins, attractive furniture, and facilities for making breakfast. On the wide first-floor landing there is a huge Murano glass chandelier and a sitting area with desk and armchairs. The topmost apartment would be perfect for a family. There is a little children's room, with two beds covered in fresh white bedspreads, and a beamed master bedroom with elegant bed and en suite bathroom, plus a kitchenette with microwave, a circular dining table, a double sofa bed and an enchanting little wooden-railed terrace with views across the rooftops to Salute. Two people could really spread out in here, and would pay only L300,000 for a night – in terms of space, a real bargain.

Nearby Bovolo Staircase; Piazza San Marco.

Calle della Madonna, San Marco 3614, 30124 Venezia
Tel (041) 5204909
Fax (041) 5204909
Location off Campo Sant' Angelo, near Teatro La Fenice; **vaporetto** Sant'Angelo
Meals breakfast (at adjacent Hotel Fenice et des Artistes)
Prices rooms L220,000– L515,000, depending on number sharing; price for 2 people sharing: L250,000– L300,000; weekly rates available

Rooms 7 suites sleeping 2–6, all with bath; all rooms have phone, TV, air-conditioning, hairdrier, safe; 6 rooms have fridge, tea/coffee making facilities
Facilities sitting area, stairlift
Credit cards AE, DC, MC, V
Children accepted
Disabled stairlift for wheelchairs to first-floor rooms
Pets not accepted
Closed Jan
Proprietor Michele Facchini

San Marco

San Gallo

All you see from the outside is a rather dilapidated cinema, but don't be put off, the entrance to the San Gallo is up a flight of stone steps and through a heavy internal door. Buzz the buzzer and you will be admitted to a room that is a breath of fresh air with not a patch of silk damask in sight. This one large room fulfils the functions of reception, sitting and breakfast areas. Although the low ceiling bristles with unstained 14thC beams, it manages to be light and airy, and is freshly decorated in white with panels of mellow *faux* marble. Smart striped sofas and chairs cluster around wooden tables, and a little bar is tucked into one corner.

The owner/manager, Luca Folin, is one of a new breed of Venetian hoteliers. Young, energetic and committed to the job, he renovated the San Gallo a year ago and really cares about his guests' comfort. He has done up the bedrooms simply, with somewhat traditional furnishings – velvet button bedheads, Murano chandeliers, busy patterned floor tiles – not so much to our taste. But there is a glorious roof terrace where in summer you can breakfast amidst the potted plants.

Nearby Piazza San Marco; San Zulian.

Campo San Gallo, San Marco 1093/a, 30124 Venezia
Tel (041) 5227311/5289877
Fax (041) 5225702
Location N of Piazza San Marco, E of Orseolo canal; **vaporetto** San Marco
Meals breakfast
Prices rooms L190,000–L425,000; standard double L290,000 (30% discount in winter); breakfast included
Rooms 12; 8 double and twin, 2 with bath, 6 with shower; 1 single, 3 triple or family, all with shower; all rooms have phone, TV, air-conditioning, minibar, hairdrier
Facilities bar/breakfast/sitting room, roof terrace
Credit cards MC, V
Children accepted
Disabled not suitable
Pets accepted
Closed never
Proprietor Luca Folin

San Marco

Town hotel

San Moisè

The interior is very Venetian, and not to everyone's taste; to us the lurid pink silk damask wallcoverings in the public rooms were more than a touch reminiscent of a high-class brothel, and the accompanying Murano glass chandeliers and wall lights appropriately garish examples of the genre. This is a matter of preference, however – some may find the decoration as elegant as it is evidently intended to be.

There are a handful of special rooms at the San Moisè – under the same ownership, and in the same mould as the Marconi (see page 44) and the San Cassiano (see page 46) – which are well worth seeking out. One has splendid carved mahogany furnishings and steps up to a little bathroom. Two others (Nos 8 and 22) have views straight down the Rio dei Barcaroli, a jolly and picturesque canal which is packed with gondolas and their camera-clicking cargo. Refurbished in 1990 in the same old-fashioned Venetian style as its sister hotels, the San Moisè struck us as being the best turned-out of the three with the friendliest staff. Its position, very central, yet tucked away at the end of a little street and on a canal, is enviable.

Nearby San Moisè; Teatro La Fenice; Piazza San Marco.

Piscina San Moisè, San Marco 2058, 30124 Venezia
Tel (041) 5203755
Fax (041) 5210670
Location off Calle Larga XXII Marzo, 2 mins walk from Piazza San Marco; **vaporetto** San Marco or water taxi
Meals breakfast
Prices rooms L115,000–L423,000; standard double L164,000–L327,000; breakfast included
Rooms 16; 13 double, twin and triple, 4 with bath, 9 with shower; 3 single, all with shower; all rooms have phone, TV, air-conditioning, minibar, hairdrier, safe
Facilities breakfast room
Credit cards AE, DC, MC, V
Children accepted
Disabled not suitable
Pets accepted
Closed never
Proprietor Franco Maschietto

San Marco

Santo Stefano

If you follow the popular route from Piazza San Marco to the Accademia gallery you will walk across the Campo Santo Stefano, a large, lively and rambling square whose church has an alarmingly tilted *campanile*.

Close to all the activity stands the Santo Stefano, a welcoming and well cared for little hotel whose front rooms have views of the square (although these are prone to noise). The hotel has long been a stalwart of our all-Italy guide, and on our latest visit we found that it had been acquired by an ambitious new owner, that prices had gone up, and that the little reception area and tiny breakfast room had been given a refreshing facelift: contemporary furniture, prettily painted ceiling beams and pillars, and marble wall panels to match the floor. Bedrooms, however, remain unchanged, and look dated and rather tired by comparison, though they have a certain sugary charm. Some are very compact, but No. 11, with views across the *campo,* is light and spacious. There is a tiny courtyard terrace at the back of the hotel as well as one in front, where you can sip a coffee and watch the world go by.

Nearby Accademia gallery; Piazza San Marco.

Campo Santo Stefano, San Marco 2957, 30124 Venezia
Tel (041) 5200166
Fax (041) 5224460
Location on large square about 500 m W of Piazza San Marco; **vaporetto** San Samuele
Meals breakfast
Prices rooms L160,000–L350,000; standard double L240,000–L350,000; breakfast included
Rooms 11; 6 double and twin, 2 single, 3 triple or quadruple, all with shower; all rooms have phone, TV, air-conditioning, minibar, hairdrier, safe
Facilities breakfast room, courtyard, lift, front terrace
Credit cards MC, V
Children accepted
Disabled access difficult
Pets accepted
Closed never
Proprietor Roberto Quatrini

San Marco

Serenissima

In our opinion, this is one of the most endearing and best-kept two-star hotels in town. Our inspector reports that she found it much more pleasurable to stay here than in many a more expensive three star, and given its central location just a few paces from the Doge's Palace, Basilica and Piazza San Marco, she deemed it value for money – a rare experience in Venice. Bedrooms are admittedly on the small side (a triple will give two people more room), but neat and pretty, some with purpose-made wooden fittings, others – the ones that have been most recently redecorated – with more attractive Venetian painted headboards, cupboards and bedside tables. The neat, tiled bathrooms have proper shower enclosures, not curtains. Try for a room with a view on to the sunny little square at the back, empty but for its central well and very peaceful. Both the charming first-floor breakfast room and white-walled corridors are hung with attractive and colourful modern paintings – these alone seem to lift the Serenissima from the rut. Downstairs in reception there is a little bar. The hotel has been looked after with great care by the same family since 1960.

Nearby Piazza San Marco; Rialto; Bovolo staircase.

Calle Goldoni, San Marco 4486, 30124 Venezia
Tel (041) 5200011
Fax (041) 5223292
Location between Piazza San Marco and Rialto, close to Calle dei Fabbri; **vaporetto** San Marco, Rialto
Meals breakfast
Prices rooms L100,000–L210,000; standard double L140,000–L210,000; breakfast included
Rooms 37; 29 double, twin and triple, 5 with bath, 24 with shower; 8 single, 2 with bath, 6 with shower; all rooms have phone, TV, air-conditioning, hairdrier
Facilities sitting area, breakfast room, bar
Credit cards AE, DC, MC, V
Children accepted
Disabled not suitable
Pets accepted
Closed after Carnival to mid-Mar
Proprietor Roberto dal Borgo

San Polo

Town guest-house

Locanda Sturion

First you have to conquer the stairs, a seemingly endless flight which rises like a ladder from the ground floor to the hotel on the third floor. The friendly receptionist must be used to her guests collapsing in front of her desk, for she refrained from smirking when this inspector presented herself gulping for air. There is no porter, but receptionists will help with luggage.

Once you have recovered sufficiently to take in your surroundings, you will find them plush. Deep red silk fabric adorns the walls in several of the bedrooms (these are non-smoking), with pale silk damask in others. Furniture throughout is walnut and mahogany, with floors of Venetian marble or covered in deep red carpet. Two rooms look on to the Grand Canal. They are spacious for two people, and can sleep two extra, one on a bed cleverly hidden during the day in a wooden box masquerading as a cupboard. A little library of guidebooks, many in English, adds a homely touch.

Locanda Sturion, found in a dark street hung with washing, has long been a hostelry. It stands on the site of a 13thC house built for foreign merchants taking their wares to the market.
Nearby Rialto; Rialto markets; Ca' d'Oro.

Calle del Storione, San Polo 679, 30125 Venezia
Tel (041) 5236243
Fax (041) 5228378
Location off Riva del Vin, close to Rialto Bridge **vaporetto** Rialto, San Silvestro
Meals breakfast
Prices rooms L220,000–L320,000; standard double L220,000–L280,000; breakfast included
Rooms 11; 8 double, twin and triple, 3 family, 10 with bath, one with shower; all rooms have phone, TV, air-conditioning, minibar, hairdrier, safe
Facilities breakfast room
Credit cards AE, MC, V
Children accepted
Disabled not suitable
Pets accepted
Closed never
Proprietor Signor Fragiacomo

San Polo

Marconi

The Marconi is a typical Venice hotel, encapsulating both what is right and what is wrong about many of them. As so often, the location is enviable (although since it is right by Rialto Bridge, overlooking a stretch of Grand Canal thick with gondolas, it appeals to those wanting action rather than peace and quiet). The building is a 16thC *palazzo* with a 19thC entrance hall which has a glass and wood frontage, marbled pillars, velvet hangings and green and gold embossed ceiling. Best of all, the two rooms with balconies which overlook the Grand Canal cost no more than the rest, so you should try hard for one of them. Bedrooms are fairly simple, but mahogany furniture, carved bedheads and damask curtains lend an old-fashioned, grandiose air. There is double glazing throughout. Yet though the hotel was renovated only in 1991, its dark wood fittings and rather dated fabrics give it a gloomy and rather musty air. And one senses that the staff, knowing that it is easy to fill the hotel, are not as interested in their guests' well-being as they might be. In other words, a hotel which lacks a heart and coasts along rather than strives. More reports please.

Nearby Rialto; Rialto markets; Ca' d'Oro.

Riva del Vin, San Polo 729, 30125 Venezia
Tel (041) 5222068
Fax (041) 5229700
Location beside Rialto Bridge, opposite the *vaporetto* landing stage **vaporetto** Rialto
Meals breakfast
Prices rooms L115,000–L327,000; standard double L164,000–L327,000; breakfast included
Rooms 28; 23 double or triple, 3 single, 2 family, all with bath or shower; all rooms have phone, TV, air-conditioning, hairdrier, safe
Facilities breakfast room, terrace
Credit cards AE, DC, MC, V
Children accepted
Disabled 1 room on ground floor
Pets accepted
Closed never
Proprietor Franco Maschietto

Santa Croce

Ai Due Fanali

A bas-relief of a saint inside the portico gives a clue to the hotel's origins as the *Scuola* of the Church of San Simeon Grande next door, in an elongated *campo* which is off the tourist track and soothingly crowd-free. By Venetian standards, this ancient building is quite unexceptional from the outside, but within, we found a glossy little hotel, stylishly furnished by its talented owner, Marina Ferron, who also owns the San Simeon Apartments (see page 128). The polished marble and stone floor of the ground-floor reception/sitting room is strewn with Persian rugs and dotted with fine antiques. The walls are hung with oil paintings and gilt-framed mirrors. Nick-nacks on the marble fireplace and fresh flowers create a homely feel .

There are great views from both the smart third-floor breakfast room (all green marble and wood) and the small roof terrace, perched on stilts on top of the building like a jetty out-of-water. Bedrooms are on the small side, but simply and tastefully decorated, with painted bedheads and modish stone-tiled bathrooms. All in all, this hotel provides Venetian sophistication without San Marco prices.

Nearby station; Scalzi; San Giacomo dell'Oro.

Campo San Simeon Grande, Santa Croce 946, 30135 Venezia
Tel (041) 718490
Fax (041) 718344
Location across the Grand Canal from the station; **vaporetto** Ferrovia or water taxi
Meals breakfast
Prices rooms L150,000–L350,000; standard double L180,000–L280,000; breakfast included
Rooms 17; 10 double and twin and triple, 7 with bath, 3 with shower; 7 single, 2 with bath, 5 with shower; all rooms have phone, TV, air-conditioning, minibar, hairdrier, safe
Facilities breakfast room, sitting area, lift, roof terrace
Credit cards AE, DC, MC, V
Children accepted
Disabled possible, but no special facilities
Pets not accepted
Closed 3 weeks in Jan
Proprietor Marina Ferron

Santa Croce

San Cassiano

Arriving by boat at San Cassiano's private jetty on the Grand Canal is considerably easier than finding your way by foot through a maze of tortuous, narrow alleyways from the nearest *vaporetto* or *traghetto* point (ask for a brochure to be sent so that you can follow its map). It also means that you can appreciate the 14thC *palazzo's* best feature: its deep red Gothic façade which faces the Grand Canal's greatest glory, the Ca' d'Oro. Inside, the hotel has a rather fusty feel to it, with heavy Venetian furnishings and a fairly lackadaisical staff – characteristics we also found in its sister hotels, the Marconi (page 44), the San Moisè (page 40) and the Ateneo (not included). Of the four, however, this one has the most grandiose rooms, and the six facing the canal are splendid, with capacious reproduction antique wardrobes, matching desks and carved bedheads, floating white curtains bordered by velvet or brocade pelmets, and oriental carpets. They are the same price as rooms without a view, and you should be tempted to look elsewhere if you can't secure one. The light, elegant breakfast room with huge windows and waterfront views is a delight.

Nearby Ca' d'Oro; Rialto Markets; Rialto Bridge.

Calle della Rosa, Santa Croce 2232, 30135 Venezia
Tel (041) 5241768
Fax (041) 721033
Location on Grand Canal, opposite Ca' d'Oro; **vaporetto** San Stae or water taxi
Meals breakfast
Prices rooms L115,000–L327,000; standard double L164,000–L327,000; breakfast included
Rooms 36; 20 double and twin, 12 triple and family, 4 single, all with bath or shower; all rooms have phone, TV, air-conditioning, minibar, hairdrier, safe
Facilities sitting room, breakfast room, bar
Credit cards AE, MC, V
Children accepted
Disabled 2 rooms specially adapted
Pets accepted
Closed never
Proprietor Franco Maschietto

Castello

Bisanzio

Our feelings about the Bisanzio are mixed. The soulless public rooms, we felt, were more suited to groups of tourists than individuals seeking character. However, the owners were planning a revamp, which may well have taken place by the time you read this. There was talk of archways and exposed beams, intimate sitting areas and marble floors. The plus here is the bedrooms, at least the good ones, which, as in many other Venice hotels, cost no more than the not-so-good ones. The latter are mainly dull boxes, the former are light and airy bargains. Best are the eight rooms with private terraces and rooftop views. No. 34, for example, has a space-enhancing lobby leading to a bathroom tiled in pale green *corto Veneziano* tiles on one side, and on the other a large terrace with views of St Mark's *campanile*. No. 82 has a smaller terrace, but the room is large and light with a capacious bath and attractive marble basin (as are all the basins in this hotel). The rooms equipped with double bed and bunk beds make an excellent choice for a family. Furnishings are mostly of the modern painted wood variety and floors and doors are insulated, cutting down outside noise to a minimum.
Nearby Riva degli Schiavoni; Piazza San Marco.

Calle de la Pietà, Castello 3651, 30122 Venezia
Tel (041) 5203100
Fax (041) 5204114
Location just off Riva degli Schiavoni, behind La Pietà **vaporetto** San Zaccaria or by water taxi
Meals breakfast
Prices rooms L180,000–L330,000; standard double L240,000–L330,000; breakfast included
Rooms 43; 37 double, twin and triple, 2 single, 4 family, 20 with bath, 23 with shower; all rooms have phone, TV, air-conditioning, minibar, hairdrier, safe
Facilities sitting room, bar, breakfast room, courtyard, lift
Credit cards AE, DC, MC, V
Children accepted
Disabled no special facilities
Pets accepted
Closed never
Proprietors Busetti family

Castello

Londra Palace

The position midway along the Riva is, of course, magnificent, with no less than 100 of the hotel's bedroom windows affording matchless views across the lagoon to the island of San Giorgio Maggiore with its perfect Palladian church of the same name. No wonder Tchaikovsky found it a congenial place in which to write his Fourth Symphony in 1877. Then there were two adjacent hotels, both opened in 1860; they merged in 1900, and in 1992 the Londra Palace was given a costly refit to create fewer, larger bedrooms. A well-known architect, Ettore Mochetti, was responsible, and one of the best features of the revamped hotel is that every room has been given the same lavish attention, so that you are unlikely to feel cheated by your allocation. The standard is high, and the quality of the Biedermeier furniture and the original paintings used throughout is exceptional. All the luxurious bathrooms have jacuzzi baths. Rooms with views over the lagoon are termed 'deluxe' and are more expensive, but the 'superior' rooms without a view are equally rich in decoration. All are subtly different; some are really lovely. The terrace restaurant, Do Leoni, makes a romantic place in which to dine.

Nearby Piazza San Marco; San Giorgio in Bragora; San Zaccaria.

Riva degli Schiavoni,
30122 Venezia
Tel (041) 5200533
Fax (041) 5225032
Location midway along the waterfront, 2 mins walk from San Marco **vaporetto** San Zaccaria, San Marco
Meals breakfast, lunch, dinner
Prices rooms L280,000–L850,000; standard double without view L310,000–L620,000; with view L460,000–L710,000; breakfast included; dinner from L100,000
Rooms 53; 33 double and twin, 20 junior suites, all with bath; all rooms have phone, TV, air-conditioning, minibar, hairdrier, safe, lift
Facilities sitting room, dining room, bar, terrace, sundeck, lift
Credit cards AE, DC, MC, V
Children accepted
Disabled no special facilities
Pets accepted
Closed never
Proprietor Ugo Samueli

Castello

La Residenza

La Residenza appeals to true lovers of Venice – the great Venice expert John Julius Norwich is a regular guest – who appreciate the chance to stay in the grand Gothic *palazzo* which dominates Campo Bandiera e Moro. Dusty and enigmatic, this quiet little square possesses one of the city's most enchanting churches, San Giovanni in Bragora, with lovely works of art.

Just to enter is an experience: press the button in the lion's mouth and huge doors swing open to reveal an ancient covered courtyard and stone steps leading up to a vast Baroque hall with beautifully coloured, lavishly carved plaster walls. Taking breakfast here in the early morning light is a rare treat. La Residenza is not, however, a grand hotel, but a modest two star in immodest surroundings, and bedrooms are a combination of grotty, kitsch, elegant and antique, mixing, for example, a superb painted Venetian wardrobe with lino floor, hideous portable air-conditioning unit, faded wallpaper, silk damask curtains and formica-covered doors. The new owner says he is intent on sensitive upgrading ... perhaps he will tackle the hotel's one drawback: a faint but pervasive smell of cats..... or is it drains?
Nearby San Giorgio degli Schiavoni; Arsenale.

Campo Bandiera e Moro, Castello 3608, 30122 Venezia
Tel (041) 5285315
Fax (041) 5885042
Location on small square 100 m behind Riva degli Schiavoni **vaporetto** Arsenale, San Zaccaria
Meals breakfast
Prices rooms L160,000–L290,000; standard double L220,000; breakfast included
Rooms 16; 13 double and twin, 2 single, 1 triple, all with bath or shower, 2 without WC; all rooms have phone, TV, air-conditioning, minibar
Facilities sitting room, breakfast area
Credit cards AE, DC, MC, V
Children accepted
Disabled not suitable
Pets accepted
Closed never
Proprietor Giovanni Ballestra

Dorsoduro

Town hotel

Accademia

Though it's not the bargain it used to be, the Accademia is still a place of immense charm with affordable prices and a convenient but calm location. What really distinguishes the *pensione* is its gardens – the large canal-side patio, where tables are scattered among plants in classical urns, and the grassy garden at the back where roses and fruit trees flourish.

Built in the 17thC as a private mansion, it retains touches of grandeur. Most of the furnishings are classically Venetian (the Murano chandeliers for once tasteful and harmonious), but there's no trace of formality. Perfect for sitting and relaxing is the finely furnished first-floor landing. The airy breakfast room has crisp white tablecloths and a beamed ceiling; but, weather permitting, guests will inevitably opt to start their day in the garden. The bedrooms have recently been renovated to a high standard with inlaid wood floors and antiqued mirrors. Work is due to start shortly on the public rooms. Our inspector found some members of staff 'charming', but others 'churlish', though the latter don't seem to deter a loyal clientele from returning here year after year.

Nearby Accademia gallery; Scuola Grande dei Carmini.

Fondamenta Bollani, Dorsoduro 1058, 30123 Venezia **Tel** (041) 5210188/5237846 **Fax** (041) 5239152 **Location** where the Toletta and Trovaso canals meet the Grand Canal; **vaporetto** Accademia or water taxi **Meals** breakfast **Prices** rooms L75,000– L260,000; standard double L180,000–L260,000; breakfast included **Rooms** 30; 22 double and twin, 9 with bath, 13 with shower; 7 single, 6 with shower; all rooms have phone, TV; most have air-conditioning, hairdrier, safe **Facilities** breakfast room, bar, sitting room, garden **Credit cards** AE, DC, MC, V **Children** accepted **Disabled** no special facilities **Pets** accepted **Closed** never **Proprietor** Stefania Salmaso

Dorsoduro

Alboretti

The Alboretti is distinguished by its warm welcome, and genuine family atmosphere. Reception is a cosy wood-panelled room with paintings of Venice on the walls and a model of a 17thC galleon in its window; the sitting room is small, but the first-floor TV room is a comfortable retreat (the TV is rarely used); the terrace behind the hotel, entirely covered by a pergola and set simply with tables and chairs, is a delight, especially for a leisurely breakfast in summer.

The style of the bedrooms is predominantly simple and modern, though a few rooms have an antique or two (such as No. 5). Like the rest of the hotel, they are well cared for and spotlessly clean, but the bathrooms are tiny, as are some of the rooms. None are large, but Nos 15, 18 and 22 are recommended for their garden view, and the former for its balcony on which you can breakfast.

Signora Linguerri runs a sophisticated restaurant next door, where you can eat in the pretty dining room or outside under the pergola; she is an expert on wine and her list offers an interesting selection.

Nearby Accademia gallery; Zattere; Gesuati.

Rio Terrà Foscarini, Dorsoduro 884, 30123 Venezia
Tel (041) 5230058
Fax (041) 5210158
Location alongside the Accademia gallery; **vaporetto** Accademia
Meals breakfast, dinner
Prices rooms L135,000–L265,000; standard double L180,000–L210,000; breakfast included; dinner from L45,000
Rooms 20; 13 double and twin, 3 with bath, 10 with shower; 6 single with shower; one family room with bath; all rooms have phone
Facilities sitting room, dining room, TV room, bar, terrace
Credit cards AE, MC, V
Children welcome
Disabled no special facilities
Pets accepted
Closed never
Proprietor Anna Linguerri

Dorsoduro

American

Set in a peaceful backwater of Dorsoduro, yet close to the Accademia and the Grand Canal, this is a quiet, dignified hotel with spacious reception rooms and a tiny terrace where you can take breakfast under a pergola in summer. The public areas have a sombre Edwardian air, with wood panelling and silk damask on the walls, tapestry or velvet upholstered chairs, Oriental rugs on Venetian mosaic floors, frilly white curtains and potted plants. Corridors are also panelled in wood, with little tables and chairs placed here and there. Bedrooms vary in size, as do the bathrooms, and though unexceptional they have pretty Venetian painted furniture (with minibars mercifully disguised as freestanding cupboards), ornate gilt mirrors and pretty Paisley-print bedspreads. Our reporter's bathroom had a black and white shower curtain covered in comical cats.

If you choose the American, you should do what you can to secure one of the nine bedrooms that overlook the canal. Nos 14 and 23 are particularly recommended, with three canal-facing French windows on two sides, and narrow balconies from where you can watch the water traffic drift by.

Nearby Accademia gallery; Zattere; Santa Maria della Salute.

Rio di San Vio, Dorsoduro 628, 30123 Venezia
Tel (041) 5204733
Fax (041) 5204048
Location midway along canal, which runs between Grand Canal and Giudecca Canal; **vaporetto** Accademia or water taxi
Meals breakfast
Prices rooms L120,000–L320,000; standard double L180,000–L300,000; canal-facing double L200,000–L320,000; breakfast included
Rooms 30 double and twin and single, 8 with bath, 22 with shower; all rooms have phone, TV, air-conditioning, minibar, hairdrier, safe
Facilities sitting area, breakfast room, terrace
Credit cards AE, MC, V
Children accepted
Disabled no special facilities
Closed never
Proprietor Salvatore Sutera Sardo

Dorsoduro

Calcina

The house where Ruskin lived is hard to resist, not only for its historical connection but for its location too, facing the sunny straits of the Giudecca canal. The simple *pensione*, inherited by a go-ahead young couple, has recently been given a facelift, and has been transformed into a stylish small hotel whose calm uncluttered rooms provide a welcome antidote to an excess of Venetian rococo.

Unlike many hotels in the city there is a marked difference in price between the rooms at the front with views across the glittering water (L240,00) and the darkish back rooms, which have no view, but are equally comfortable (L170,000). Most expensive are the corner rooms (L280,000), where the sun streams in from two directions. None of the rooms are large, but all compensate with cool cream walls, warm parquet floors, antiques and gleaming bathrooms. A buffet breakfast is served in summer on a large floating terrace (or you can book the romantic roof garden for two), and in winter in a marble-floored bar with a picture window, so that even if you opt for a bedroom at the back you can still enjoy the vista.

Nearby Gesuati church; Accademia gallery.

Fondamenta Zattere ai Gesuati, Dorsoduro 780, 30123 Venezia
Tel (041) 5206466
Fax (041) 5227045
Location on W side of San Vio canal; **vaporetto** Zattere or water taxi
Meals breakfast
Prices rooms L90,000–L280,000; standard double L170,000–L240,000; breakfast included
Rooms 29; 22 double and twin, 2 with bath, 20 with shower; 7 single, 1 with bath, 3 with shower, 3 with washbasin; all rooms have phone, air-conditioning, hairdrier, safe
Facilities breakfast room/bar, sitting area, terrace, roof terrace
Credit cards AE, DC, MC, V
Children accepted
Disabled not suitable
Pets not accepted
Closed never
Proprietors Alessandro and Debora Szemere

Dorsoduro

Locanda Ca' Foscari

You will need help finding Calle Frescada, a little lane tucked almost out of sight and unmarked on most maps: take Calle Larga Foscari towards the Frari, and at the junction with Crosera, turn right. Calle Frescada runs across the end, and the hotel faces down Crosera. Happily our inspector's maddening search for this little one-star hotel was worth the effort – Ca' Foscari is a cut above. Somehow its charming, modest exterior – smart front door and bell pull, little lantern displaying its name – tells the story, and the interior does not disappoint, nor the welcome from Valter and Giuliana Scarpa.

On the ground floor is a little breakfast room. A couple of flights of stairs, and you are in a fresh, white corridor with white-painted doors leading to the bedrooms. These are modest, as you would expect, but pristine, with lacy curtains and pretty bedspreads and white-tiled minute bathrooms, or, in rooms without bathrooms, decent basins. Note that the communal bathroom only has a shower, not a bath. The metal-framed beds are much more comfortable than they look. An excellent budget hotel in a bustling residential neighbourhood.

Nearby Scuola Grande di San Rocco; Frari; Accademia gallery.

Calle della Frescada, Dorsoduro 3888-3887/b, 30123 Venezia
Tel (041) 710401/710817
Fax (041) 710817
Location between Campo San Tomà and Palazzi Foscari; **vaporetto** San Tomà
Meals breakfast
Prices rooms L80,000–L160,000; standard double L130,000; breakfast included
Rooms 11; 6 double and twin, 3 with shower, 3 with basin only; 1 single with shower; 2 triples without shower; 2 family rooms without shower; communal bathroom with shower
Facilities breakfast room
Credit cards MC, V
Children accepted
Disabled not suitable
Pets accepted
Closed 15 Nov to Feb
Proprietor Valter Scarpa

Dorsoduro

Pausania

The San Barnaba area, traditionally the home of impecunious Venetian nobility, is quiet and picturesque, and now highly desirable as the better-known San Marco district becomes increasingly tourist-ridden and overpriced. The Pausania is a small hotel lying close to the last surviving floating vegetable shop in Venice – a colourful barge on the San Barnaba canal.

The building is quintessentially Venetian, a weathered Gothic *palazzo* with distinctive ogee windows. Inside, timbered ceilings, Corinthian columns, an ancient well-head and a battered but beautiful stone staircase are features of the original building. Bedrooms are all decorated in the same tastefully restrained style, combining restful blues and creamy yellows. A recent reporter complains of the lack of drawer space, but this is a problem common to many Venetian hotels. Breakfast is served in an airy modern extension overlooking a secluded garden. Unusually for such a small hotel, there are several comfortable places to sit, including a sunny canal-side landing with floor-to-ceiling windows, a beamy reception area and bar. Staff are cheerful and friendly.

Nearby Scuola Grande dei Carmini; Accademia gallery.

Fondamenta Gherardini, Dorsoduro 2824, 30123 Venezia
Tel (041) 5222083
Fax (041) 5222989
Location just W of Campo San Barnaba on San Barnaba canal; **vaporetto** Ca' Rezzonico or water taxi
Meals breakfast
Prices rooms L120,000–L450,000; standard double L200,000–L310,000; breakfast included
Rooms 31; 23 double and twin, 3 single, 5 family, all with bath or shower; all rooms have phone, TV, air-conditioning, minibar, hairdrier
Facilities sitting room, bar, breakfast room, garden
Credit cards AE, MC, V
Children accepted
Disabled no special facilities, but some rooms on ground floor
Pets accepted
Closed never
Proprietor Guido Gatto

Dorsoduro

Salute da Cici

A long-time favourite of ours, this calm, civilized hotel inhabits a *palazzo* on a small canal in an interesting area between the Accademia and Salute. If you've had your fill of baroque churches, it's also perfectly placed for a visit to the Guggenheim Collection and a blast of abstract expressionism.

The façade is charming and typically Venetian: peeling stucco and rose-coloured brick, Gothic windows and stone balconies decked with flowers. And the interior doesn't disappoint. It has a classically elegant lobby of columns and marble floors beneath exposed rafters. A little bar is reserved for guests, and a tiny, sheltered garden offers a few sunny tables for a drink. Interconnecting basement rooms, dating from the time when this was a *pensione*, provide breakfast areas. Corridors lead off a beautifully furnished first-floor landing to simple white-painted bedrooms with high ceilings, Venetian marble floors and furniture that ranges from antique to utility. There's no difference in price, so request a room on the canal or, if you're willing to sacrifice character for comfort, go for one of the nine modern rooms in the annexe.

Nearby Guggenheim Collection; Santa Maria della Salute.

Fondamenta di Ca' Balla , Dorsoduro 222, 30123 Venezia
Tel (041) 5235404
Fax (041) 5222271
Location just S of Rio Calle Terra Nuovo, 5 mins walk E of Salute; **vaporetto** Salute or water taxi
Meals breakfast
Prices rooms L90,000–L330,000; standard double L180,000 (10% discount in low season); breakfast included
Rooms 50 double and twin, single, triple and family, 41 with bath or shower; phones planned for rooms
Facilities bar, sitting area, breakfast room, garden
Credit cards not accepted
Children accepted
Disabled not suitable
Pets not accepted
Closed mid-Nov to Christmas, Jan to Mar (or Carnival if earlier)
Proprietor Sebastiano Cagnin

Dorsoduro

Seguso

Sitting on the wide sunny promenade of the Zattere, lapped by the choppy waters of the wide Giudecca canal, gives you the distinct feeling of being by the seaside. This open setting, with a grand panorama across the lagoon, is just one of the charms of the Seguso. A *pensione* in the old tradition, it is family-run, friendly and solidly old-fashioned. And (unlike most hotels in Venice) prices are modest; the Seguso is not noted for its food, but half-board here costs no more than bed and breakfast alone in hotels of similar comfort closer to San Marco.

The best bedrooms are the large ones at the front of the house, overlooking the canal – though for the privilege of the views and space you may have to forfeit the luxury of a private bathroom (only half the rooms have their own facilities). The main public rooms are the dining room, prettily furnished in traditional style, and the modest sitting room where you can sink into large leather chairs and peruse ancient editions of travel writing and guidebooks. Breakfast is taken on the front terrace – delightful. Fellow guests are often friendly, interesting and great Venice enthusiasts.

Nearby Accademia gallery; Gesuati church.

Zattere ai Gesuati, Dorsoduro 779, 30123 Venezia
Tel (041) 5222340/5286858
Fax (041) 5222340
Location 5 mins walk S of Accademia, overlooking Giudecca canal; **vaporetto** Zattere or water taxi
Meals breakfast, lunch, dinner
Prices half board (lunch or dinner) L220,000–L310,000; standard double with half board L310,000; breakfast included
Rooms 36; 31 double and twin, 5 single, 9 with bath, 9 with shower; all rooms have phone
Facilities dining room, sitting room, lift, terrace
Credit cards AE, MC, V
Children accepted
Disabled access possible
Pets accepted
Closed Dec to Feb
Proprietors Seguso family

Cannaregio

Club Cristal

The setting could hardly be more ideal, at least for those seeking a peaceful backwater: an airy, palatial town house overlooking a tree-lined courtyard and a little canal in a quiet residential corner of Cannaregio, yet only five minutes' walk from the Ca' d'Oro. It is the family home of Susan Schiavon, an Englishwoman ("not *pure* English; lots of other nationalities come into it besides") who has lived in Venice for many years and now lets five of its bedrooms to discerning visitors for whom she is a fund of knowledge about the city.

An elegant white marble staircase leads to the *piano nobile* and a high-ceilinged sitting room filled with books and squashy sofas and armchairs. A perfect breakfast is served on the plant-filled terrace beyond. The bedrooms, entered through original doors painted with birds and flowers, vary in size, some large; all are full of character, with family furniture, comfortable beds, and crisp linen. Susan serves dinner by arrangement, and you should take advantage of her accomplished home cooking at least once. Take note that Club Cristal is emphatically a home, not a hotel; couples often return, and lone women feel particularly at ease. **Nearby** Gesuiti; Ca' d'Oro; Rialto.

For further information all nationalities should contact: Liz Heavenstone, 190 Regent's Park Road, London NW1 8XP, England **Tel** (London) 0171 722 7139 **Fax** 0171 586 3004 **Location** on a small canal, between Ca' d'Oro; and Gesuiti **vaporetto** Ca' d'Oro, Fondamente Nuove **Meals** breakfast, dinner by arrangement **Prices** rooms (payable to London office in sterling only) £50–£120; standard double £100–£120; single night supplement; dinner £25 (including wine); breakfast included **Rooms** 4 double, 1 single, all with bath or shower; all rooms have hairdrier **Facilities** sitting room, dining room, terrace **Credit cards** AE, D **Children** preferred over 12 years old **Disabled** not suitable **Pets** not accepted **Closed** never **Proprietor** Susan Schiavon

Cannaregio

Locanda Ai Santi Apostoli

Be on the lookout for a pair of handsome dark green doors which herald the discreet entrance of this converted *palazzo*. Beyond is a scruffy courtyard and a quirky lift that takes you up to the third floor. What lies in store for you here is totally unexpected: a lovely apartment that has been transformed by the Bianchi Michiel family into an elegant, if pricey, B&B. The sitting room is the epitome of style: oil paintings hang on glossy apricot walls; heavy lamps rest on antique tables; sofas and chairs are covered in quiet chintz or swathed in calico. At the far end, a triptych of wood-framed windows overlooks the Grand Canal. Ornaments and books left casually around make it feel more like a home than a hotel.

Large and individually decorated, the bedrooms have been done out recently in glazed chintzes and stunning strong colours. Like the sitting room, they are dotted with antiques and pretty china nick-nacks. The two on the Grand Canal are considerably dearer than the rest. Stefano also owns a one-bedroom apartment on the second floor, with a vibrant green colour scheme, no view of the canal, but a sunny roof terrace.

Nearby Ca' d'Oro; Santi Apostoli; Miracoli.

Strada Nova, Cannaregio 4391, 30131 Venezia
Tel (041) 5212612
Fax (041) 5212611
Location just E of Campo Santi Apostoli; **vaporetto** Ca' d'Oro
Meals breakfast
Prices rooms L320,000–L500,000; standard double L320,000–L420,000; apartment prices on request; breakfast included
Rooms 11 double and twin, 6 with bath, 4 with shower; all rooms have phone, TV, air-conditioning, minibar, hairdrier
Facilities breakfast room, sitting room, lift
Credit cards AE, DC, MC, V
Children accepted
Disabled not suitable
Pets accepted
Closed Jan, 2–3 weeks in Aug, sometimes 2 weeks in Dec
Proprietor Stefano Bianchi Michiel

Cannaregio

Town hotel

Locanda di Orsaria

In a street with its fair share of hotels, the Locanda di Orsaria is by far the smallest and by far the most charming. The front door, flanked by bay trees, leads straight into a pretty, beamed reception-cum-breakfast room, which, though the size of a shoebox, seats 12 for a slap-up buffet breakfast each morning. Wooden furniture, fresh flowers and a tapestry hung on a wall lend a country air, echoed upstairs in the simply, yet tastefully furnished bedrooms. We were amazed and pleased by their size in comparison with the ground floor. The windows are big too, and – of great significance in summer – this is the only hotel in Venice, the owner claims, where all the rooms have mosquito screens. Terracotta floors and white-painted walls, both upstairs and down, loose-weave chintz bedspreads, and attractive plain wood furniture (we loved the 'dressing chests') mark the style as more Tuscan than Venetian.

Ironically, presiding over this diminutive gem is a larger-than-life character, the ebullient Renato Polesel: a genial host, who seldom seems to leave his post in reception and is always eager to help his guests.

Nearby station; Scalzi; Palazzo Labia; San Geremia.

Calle Priuli, Cannaregio 103, 30121 Venezia
Tel (041) 715254
Fax (041) 715433
Location next to the station, to the E; **vaporetto** Ferrovia
Meals breakfast
Prices rooms L140,000–L310,000; standard double L140,000–L260,000; breakfast included
Rooms 8; 5 double and twin, 3 triple, all with shower; all rooms have phone, TV, air-conditioning, minibar, hairdrier, safe
Facilities breakfast room
Credit cards AE, DC, MC, V
Children accepted
Disabled 1 room on ground floor
Pets accepted
Closed 3 weeks at beginning of Dec
Proprietor Renato Polesel

Lagoon Islands

Ca' del Borgo

If you are looking for somewhere calm and refined in which to install a group of friends, Ca' del Borgo could be an answer; as well as operating as an ordinary hotel, it is particularly well suited to private parties.

Ca' del Borgo stands in a wide, quiet street in Malamocco. A handsome town house, it was renovated a few years ago for private use, and then sold to the present hotelier owners. It retains the air of a gracious and civilized home, with eight spacious, comfortable and smartly decorated bedrooms with a large terrace and a little garden with a stone well. A grandiose entrance hall with beamed ceiling and oriental rugs sets the tone. Bedrooms have parquet floors, oriental rugs, excellent beds, perhaps deep red silk damask on the walls, perhaps a colour scheme of yellow and blue. Bathrooms are marble, with efficient showers. Service is discreet.

A car would be useful. The hotel is out of the way, and it could transport guests to the Ca' del Moro sports and health club, which they are entitled to use; they also have use of the Hotel Excelsior's beach. Free bikes are provided.

Nearby Venice; Lagoon Islands.

Piazza delle Erbe, Malamocco, Lido, 30126 Venezia
Tel (041) 770749
Fax (041) 770799
Location in Malamocco village, 6 km SW of Lido; parking
vaporetto Santa Maria Elisabetta then taxi or hotel minibus, or by hotel water taxi
Meals breakfast
Prices rooms L200,000–L490,000; breakfast included
Rooms 8 double and twin, 3 with bath (2 with jacuzzi bath), 5 with shower; all rooms have phone, TV, air-conditioning, minibar, hairdrier, safe
Facilities sitting room, breakfast room, terrace; catering facilities available
Credit cards AE, DC, MC, V
Children accepted
Disabled one specially adapted room on ground floor
Pets accepted
Closed Dec, Jan
Proprietor Signor Vianello

Lagoon Islands

Locanda Cipriani

We do not apologize for including the Locanda Cipriani, even though its rooms are, as we write, closed, and may never open again. A planning dispute has caused the problem, but we hope that by the time you read this they are once more open, because they are amongst the loveliest in this guide. In the meantime, you can still eat in the restaurant, although on our visits we found the food disappointing and the prices high.

Torcello is the cradle of the Venetian civilization, yet all that remains are two serenely beautiful churches, Santa Fosca and the ancient cathedral, the last with its haunting Byzantine mosaic of the Madonna. When the crowds drift home, Torcello's magic begins to work, and only the Locanda's guests are privileged to witness it. These have included Hemingway, Chaplin, Paul Newman and the entire British royal family. The rooms in which they stayed are simple and homely yet sophisticated, with polished wood floors, attractive pictures on white walls, writing desks, *objets d'art*, comfortable sofas and armchairs. As the owner, grandson of its founder Harry Cipriani, says, their closure would be a loss to Venice.

Nearby Venice (40 mins); Lagoon Islands.

Torcello, 30012 Burano, Venezia
Tel (041) 730150
Fax (041) 735433
Location in centre of island, overlooking the cathedral; **vaporetto** Torcello
Meals breakfast, lunch, dinner
Prices half board L260,000 per person
Rooms 6; 3 double with sitting rooms, 3 single, all with bath; all rooms have phone
Facilities sitting room, dining room, bar, terrace, garden
Credit cards AE, MC, V
Children accepted
Disabled not suitable
Pets accepted
Closed Nov to mid-Mar
Proprietor Bonifacio Brass

Lagoon Islands

Seaside hotel, Lido

Quattro Fontane

The longer we lingered at the Quattro Fontane, the more it grew on us. At first the 150-year-old mock Tyrolean building struck us as rather gloomy and suburban, but we soon warmed to the charmingly decorated reception rooms, particularly the *salone* and the little writing room. Mementos of the owners' travels are dotted around the hotel on walls and shelves – carved wooden figures, painted shells, model ships, porcelain, stamps. In the baronial dining room, with its cavernous hearth and bold red chairs, service was directed with courtesy by the long-serving head waiter. In warm weather you can eat on the wide tree-filled terrace that encircles the hotel.

The bedrooms in the main building have plenty of character and are individually decorated with an assortment of furniture, pictures and fabrics, comfortable if not luxurious. Those in the 1960s annexe are more streamlined, but here too each is different, attractive and cosy, with gaily tiled bathrooms. A dignified hotel, elderly now, but still spruce, and in our opinion the best on the Lido. Only giggling, secretly smoking chambermaids let the side down on our visit.

Nearby Venice; Lagoon Islands.

Via Quattro Fontane 16,
30126 Lido, Venezia
Tel (041) 5260227
Fax (041) 5260726
Location set back from seafront on S side of Lido, near Casino; **vaporetto** Santa Maria Elisabetta
Meals breakfast, lunch, dinner
Prices rooms L260,000–L480,000; standard double L350,000; breakfast included; dinner from L60,000
Rooms 58; 54 double, 4 single, 35 with bath, 23 with shower; all rooms have phone, TV, air-conditioning, hairdrier, safe
Facilities sitting room, writing room, dining room, bar; tennis court and beach cabins available
Credit cards AE, DC, MC, V
Children accepted
Disabled access difficult
Pets accepted
Closed Nov to Easter
Proprietor Bevilacqua family

Lagoon Islands

Restaurant-with-rooms, Burano

Al Raspo de Ua

If you want an interesting experience, local colour, and indeed charm at probably the lowest price in the Venetian Lagoon, then this could be it. And Venice is only a 40-minute *vaporetto* ride away.(The photograph shows Burano's waterfront.)

Al Raspo de Ua is a restaurant at the heart of the meltingly pretty island of Burano, with its brightly daubed little houses, on a pedestrian thoroughfare, close to a canal. To be truthful, it is flanked by souvenir shops and picture postcard stands, but the restaurant itself is bustling and well turned out, clearly the most popular on the island, packed at lunchtime in season. The back room, hung with fishing nets, has its share of character, and the staff, when we visited, seemed to be good types.

When evening comes, and the day trippers depart to the city, the charm should start to work its spell. This is no more, or less, than a simple restaurant with rooms to let above (the only facility for lodgers, apart from the bedrooms, is a separate side entrance for their use) but the rooms are cheerful enough, clean, and fairly recently equipped, with just one communal bathroom. This place is a well-kept secret: make sure you book well ahead.
Nearby Venice; Lagoon Islands.

Via Galuppi 560, Burano, 30012 Venezia
Tel (041) 730095
Fax (041) 730397
Location at centre of island, on pedestrian thoroughfare, 5 mins walk from landing stage; **vaporetto** Burano
Meals breakfast, lunch, dinner
Prices double L80,000; breakfast included; dinner from L30,000
Rooms 5 double; one communal bathroom with shower only, plus one further WC
Facilities dining room, sitting area
Credit cards AE, DC, MC, V
Children accepted
Disabled not suitable
Pets accepted
Closed Jan; restaurant closed Wed
Proprietors Mario Bruzzese and Giuliano Padouan

Lagoon Islands

Villa Mabapa

Set peacefully in a garden overlooking the lagoon, Villa Mabapa has been included in our all-Italy guide for several years, and warmly recommended. A recent visit, however, left our inspector less than enthusiastic, her main criticisms being the cool, dismissive attitude of the reception staff and management, the dowdy decoration and the banal food.

The hotel consists of two buildings. The Villa itself, built as a family home in the 1930s, contains the high-ceilinged public rooms and some traditional-style bedrooms. The best are on the first floor. Our inspector reports that hers, although a lovely room with a huge sweep of windows overlooking the lagoon, was haphazardly furnished and felt rather bare. The bedrooms in the annexe are very dull, and all the same. In between the two buildings is a garden which is overlooked by the long dining room; however, the best place to eat, weather permitting, is on the terrace, with wonderful sunset views.

And the name? It consists of the first syllables of the words *mamma*, *bambino*, and *papà*. These days, it is the *bambino* who is in charge.

Nearby Venice; Lagoon Islands.

Riviera San Nicolò 16, Lido, 30126 Venezia
Tel (041) 5260590
Fax (041) 5269441
Location on Lagoon side of the Lido, 15 mins walk from Santa Maria Elisabetta landing stage; in gardens; parking **vaporetto** San Nicolò (infrequent stop), Santa Maria Elisabetta or by water taxi **Meals** breakfast, lunch, dinner **Prices** rooms L100,000–L450,000; standard double L190,000–L300,000; breakfast included; dinner from L30,000 **Rooms** 60; 44 double and twin, 15 single, 1 suite, all with bath or shower; all rooms have phone, TV, air-conditioning, hairdrier, safe **Facilities** sitting room, breakfast room, dining room, bar, lift, terrace, garden **Credit cards** AE, DC, MC, V **Children** accepted **Disabled** some rooms on ground floor **Pets** accepted **Closed** sometimes Jan **Proprietor** Signor Vianello

Veneto

Country villa, Arcugnano

Villa Michelangelo

Much of the southern Veneto countryside is flat and industrial-ized and the undulating vine-clad slopes of Monte Berico make not only a pleasant contrast but also an attractive central base for visiting Verona, Padua and Vicenza. Villa Michelangelo has the further advantage of a peaceful setting, wide views and a pool with sliding glass roof overlooking the hills. If it had more char-acter it would be perfect.

The severe-looking 18thC villa was a Capuchin college before it became a hotel, and there is a simplicity about its decorative style even now. The dining room is elegant, with white walls, sparkling white Murano glass chandeliers suspended from a roughly beamed ceiling, a wall of glass doors leading to the ter-race, and great vases of perfumed flowers. The food served here is fancy Italian which doesn't always come off. Bedrooms are fair-ly uniform, comfortable enough but unmemorable. Bathrooms have large green marble basins and proper towels.

Reached from the lobby by a tunnel, the conference centre, along with the pool and piano bar, is cleverly positioned so that the tranquility of the hotel remains undisturbed.

Nearby Vicenza (7 km); Verona (40 km); Padua (40 km).

Via Sacco 19, 36057 Arcugnano, Vicenza
Tel (0444) 550300
Fax (0444) 550490
Location 7 km S of Vicenza, signposted from Arcugnano, in own park with ample parking
Meals breakfast, lunch, dinner
Prices rooms L190,000–L410,000; standard double L270,000–L310,000; breakfast included; dinner from L60,000
Rooms 54; 34 double and twin, 15 single, 2 family, 3 suites, all with bath or shower; all rooms have phone, TV, air-conditioning, minibar, hairdrier
Facilities dining room, piano bar, terrace, pool, conference room, lift
Credit cards AE, DC, MC, V
Children accepted
Disabled two rooms specially adapted
Pets accepted
Closed never
Manager Sebastiano Leder

Veneto

Town hotel, Asolo

Al Sole

From a glorious position, perched above the Piazza Maggiore on the steep hill up to the massive fortress, the Rocca, this *albergo* has a splendid view of the medieval town with its higgledy-piggledy streets. Its deep pink façade is original and appealing, while the trendy interior – hallmark of the dynamic young owner Silvia de Checchi – affords a dramatic contrast.

Almost every room has white rough-cast walls and mellow wood floors, enlivened by daring colour combinations for fabrics and furniture. Although the look is mainly cool and modern, a few antiques and the occasional bowl and pitcher hark back to the past. Recalling former stars in Asolo's firmament, such as 'Eleanor Duse' and 'Gabriele D'Annunzio', the bedrooms are all different; the former has light painted furniture, the latter, ornate church-style pieces. Some rooms have huge claw-foot baths; some have massage showers, just one of the many four-star comforts. Perhaps the ultimate of these is the state-of-the-art downstairs lavatory, which electronically flushes, lifts and then replaces the seat, complete with hygenic paper cover, at the appropriate times.

Nearby Palladian villas; Possagno (10 km).

Via Collegio 33, 31011 Asolo, Treviso
Tel (0423) 528111
Fax (0423) 528399
Location at the top of Piazza Maggiore; private car park
Meals breakfast
Prices rooms L150,000–L450,000; standard double L250,000–L350,000; breakfast included
Rooms 23; 14 double and twin, 2 with bath, 12 with shower; 8 single, 2 with bath, 6 with shower; 1 suite with bath; all rooms have phone, TV, air-conditioning, minibar, hairdrier, safe
Facilities breakfast room, sitting room, sitting area, bar, meeting room, lift, terrace
Credit cards AE, MC, V
Children accepted
Disabled 2 specially adapted rooms
Pets accepted
Closed never
Proprietor Silvia de Checchi

Veneto

Villa Cipriani

Asolo is a beautiful medieval hilltop village commanding panoramic views, a jewel of the Veneto. The Villa Cipriani, a jewel of the huge ITT Sheraton Group, is a mellow ochre-washed house on the fringes of the village, its deceptively plain entrance leading into a warm reception area which immediately imparts the feeling of a hotel with a heart (and a house with a past: it was once the home of Robert Browning). Today it is graced by the prettiest of rose-and-flower-filled gardens, and delicious meals are served on the terrace or in the restaurant overhanging the valley. As for the gracious and comfortable bedrooms, make sure you ask for one with a view, and try for an 'exclusive' rather than a 'superior' double. The latter are not particularly spacious, while the former include a sitting area; two rooms have terraces.

Villa Cipriani is a relaxing country hotel, whose views, comfort, peaceful garden and good food make it particularly alluring. However, some reports complain of prices that were hard to justify, also mentioning intrusive wedding parties and brash clientele. Others have been full of praise.

Nearby Palladian villas; Possagno (10 km).

Via Canova 298, 31011 Asolo, Treviso
Tel (0423) 952166
Fax (0423) 952095
Location on NW side of village; with garage parking
Meals breakfast, lunch, dinner
Prices rooms L270,000–L550,000; 'superior' double L360,000; 'exclusive' double L460,000; terrace room L550,000; breakfast L26,000; dinner from L80,000. All prices plus 10% VAT

Rooms 31; 29 double and twin, 2 single, all with bath; all rooms have phone, TV, air-conditioning, minibar, hairdrier
Facilities sitting room, dining rooms, bar, meeting room, lift, terrace, garden
Credit cards AE, DC, MC, V
Children accepted
Disabled access difficult
Pets accepted
Closed never
Manager Gianpaolo Burattin

Veneto

Il Castello

Il Castello refers to a handsome villa built in the 15thC on the ruins of an ancient castle which looks down over the medieval village of Barbarano. Occupied for the last century by the Marinoni family, it retains the original perimeter walls of the castle, and its cellars. There is a Renaissance garden and a citrus garden, the lemon trees standing in rows of terracotta pots. To the south stretches the family's vineyard; *grappa,* olive oil and honey are also produced.

As you enter Il Castello through stone gates and a cobbled, covered way, the family villa is on the right, and the guest house ahead, overlooking a large walled courtyard. Adjacent is a converted barn, used for concerts, exhibitions and wedding parties. The guest house can be taken as one house or two separate apartments, each sleeping up to six people, both with kitchens and bathrooms. Rooms, white-painted and airy, with Venetian marble floors, are somewhat spartan in feel, despite the use of old family furniture throughout. There are two communal rooms, one with a fireplace, where guests can meet and chat if they like. English is spoken.

Nearby Vicenza (22 km); Padua (32 km); Verona (34 km).

Via Castello 6, 36021
Barbarano, Vicenza
Tel (0444) 886055
Fax (0444) 886055
Location on S side of Barbarano; follow signs to Il Castello in village; in own grounds with secure parking
Meals none
Prices rooms L35,000 per night per adult; L30,000 per night per child under 12; bookings not less than 7 nights in high season (July, Aug, Christmas, Easter) and 3 nights in low season; reduced rates available for stays over 7 nights in low season; heating extra
Rooms two apartments with kitchen and bathroom each sleeping up to 6 people
Facilities garden, produce shop
Credit cards not accepted
Children welcome
Disabled access possible
Closed never
Proprietor Elda Marinoni and family

Veneto

Town hotel, Cortina d'Ampezzo

Menardi

Old black-and-white photographs are evidence of how this family-run hotel on the northern side of Cortina has evolved. Built as a home in 1836 on the main highway connecting the Kingdom of Italy with the Hapsburg Empire, it became a coaching inn when its owners, the Menardi family, began hiring out horses and then providing rough and ready accommodation for weary travellers. During the First World War, Luigi Menardi found himself working as a porter in a Florence hotel, and when he returned to the mountains, began to transform the rustic inn into a proper hotel. Today the long white building has proliferated carved green wood balconies and tumbling geraniums, plus an extra line of rooms sprouting from the roof and a separate annexe behind, but the Menardi family can still justifiably proclaim: 'same house, same family, same relaxed atmosphere'. Inside, antique pieces, painted religious statues and old work tools are mixed with local custom-made furnishings which look somewhat dated but are nonetheless comfortable. The atmosphere is one of traditional warmth and service is polished. The large garden is a secluded delight.
Nearby skiing; Dolomites; Belluno (71 km).

Via Majon 110, 32043 Cortina d'Ampezzo, Belluno
Tel (0436) 2400
Fax (0436) 862183
Location on SS51, on northern side of Cortina; in large grounds with private parking
Meals breakfast, lunch, dinner
Prices rooms L110,000–L340,000; standard double L180,000–L330,000; breakfast included; dinner from L35,000
Rooms 51 double and twin, single and family rooms, all with bath; all rooms have phone, TV, hairdrier
Facilities sitting room, dining room, bar, garden
Credit cards AE, DC, MC, V
Children accepted
Disabled access difficult
Pets not accepted
Closed Oct to mid-Dec, mid-Apr to mid-Jun
Proprietors Menardi family

Veneto

Villa Saraceno

Highlights of the Veneto are the villas built by the great Renaissance architect Andrea Palladio. If you would like to stay in one, here is your chance. Villa Saraceno, on a plain to the west of the Euganean Hills, is owned by the Landmark Trust, a British organization which acquires and restores buildings of historic interest and then lets them to holidaymakers.

Designed in the mid-16thC as a country retreat as well as working farm for a well-to-do Vicenzan, Biagio Saraceno, the complex consists of the airy, beautifully proportioned main house as well as other earlier buildings, including the simple Casa Vecchia, in which most of the bedrooms are located. The interior of the Palladian house has been restored to recreate its original arrangement – a grand *sala* with two-room apartments opening off it and huge granaries above. Dim frescoed friezes have been cleaned to reveal scenes of high drama, probably painted for Biagio's son. Saraceno can accommodate up to 16 people. One recent tenant wrote to the Landmark Trust: 'a perfect balance between the elegant understatement of the Palladian building and the comfort of the 1990s ... '

Nearby Montagnana (14 km); Vicenza (32 km).

Via Finale 8, 36020 Agugliaro, Vicenza. For all information and booking contact: The Landmark Trust, Shottesbrooke, Maidenhead, Berkshire SL6 3SW, England **Tel** (Landmark Trust) 01628 825925 **Fax** (Landmark Trust) 01628 825417 **Location** in village 32 km S of Vicenza, 12 km N of SS10 between Este and Montagnana **Meals** none **Prices** weekly rates for villa from £988 to £4,309 depending on dates; weekly lets only available in high season, shorter stays available at other times **Rooms** accommodates up to 16 in 2 double, 3 twin, 2 single, 1 family room; 5 bathrooms **Facilities** kitchen with dishwasher and washing machine, sitting room, dining room, garden, swimming pool **Credit cards** MC, V **Children** accepted **Disabled** access difficult **Pets** accepted **Closed** never

Veneto

Abbazia

The hotel consists of two buildings: a 17thC *palazzo* and, adjacent, an enchanting little art nouveau villa. Standards of decoration and comfort in both are exceptionally high – rarely have we met hoteliers (brother and sister) more keen to please their guests. If you find the lobby and balconied breakfast area a bit much – a sugary pink confection of candy-striped walls strewn with roses, draped tables and floral china – you will not be disappointed by the bedrooms. Each one is individually decorated, and all are delightful: sophisticated and very feminine in English style, full of thoughtful touches. Three rooms have private balconies, at no extra cost. Best of all is the villa with its pillared portico, carved flourishes on its four façades and sweeping staircase. Here you could choose the Richard Attenborough or the Sandra Bullock suite, named in honour of the stars who were resident while filming *In Love and War*.

The owners have prepared a helpful list of local information, including routes which you can follow on the hotel's bicycles. There are two superb restaurants nearby: Da Lino in Solighetto (see page 85) and Da Gigetto in Miane.

Nearby 11thC abbey; Palladian villas; Asolo (20 km).

Via Martiri della Libertà,
31051 Follina, Treviso
Tel (0438) 971277
Fax (0438) 970001
Location in town centre, facing the abbey; parking
Meals breakfast
Prices rooms L120,000–L380,000; standard double L200,000; breakfast L20,000
Rooms 24; 16 double and twin, one single, 7 suites, all with shower, bath or jacuzzi bath; all rooms have phone, TV, hairdrier; 12 have air-conditioning and safe
Facilities breakfast room, terrace, sitting room, tea room, garden
Credit cards AE, DC, MC, V
Children accepted
Disabled not suitable
Pets not accepted
Closed never
Proprietors Giovanni and Ivana Zanon

Veneto

Country villa apartments, Gargagnago

Foresteria Serègo Alighieri

In 1353, the son of Dante, who had been exiled in Verona, bought Casal dei Ronchi, and there his direct descendants have lived ever since. Today, overseen by Count Pieralvise Serègo Alighieri, the estate is a prosperous producer of Valpolicella wines (much improved in recent years and shaking off their 'cheap and nasty' reputation) as well as olive oil, balsamic vinegar, honey, jams and rice. The family home is a lovely yellow ochre building fronted by formal gardens which overlook the vineyards. Beyond are the former stables, now beautifully converted to make eight apartments, simple yet sophisticated, sleeping two to four people. In each one you find a gleaming chrome kitchen, country furniture, soothing green cotton fabrics, white walls, marble bathrooms. No. 8 spirals up a slim tower: minute sitting room, stairs to a minute kitchen, more stairs to the bedroom. Open a door in the bedhead and there's a tiny window behind. No. 1 is the most spacious, with dining table and elegant chairs. Breakfast is served in a room decorated with old family photographs on the ground floor. There are some good restaurants nearby.

Nearby Verona (18 km); Lake Garda (14 km).

37020 Gargagnago di Valpolicella, Verona
Tel (045) 7703622
Fax (045) 7703523
Location signposted off the road from Pedemonte to San Ambrogio, 18 km NE of Verona; in own extensive grounds with ample parking
Meals breakfast
Prices apartment sleeping 2–4 people from L200,000 to L480,000 per night; weekly rates available; breakfast

L12,000
Rooms 8 apartments for 2, 3 or 4 people, each with kitchen, bathroom with shower, phone, TV, air-conditioning
Facilities reception, breakfast room, terrace, meeting room, estate produce shop
Credit cards AE, MC, V
Children accepted
Disabled not suitable
Pets accepted **Closed** Jan
Proprietor Conte Pieralvise Serègo Alighieri

Veneto

Agriturismo, Levada

Gargan

The setting is rural, on a working farm, and the farmhouse is typical – attractive enough, but not especially prepossessing. A donkey brays in the garden. We walked in quite unprepared for the level of sophistication of this *agriturismo*; it's in a league of its own. The ground floor comprises a hallway with cool white walls and beams painted pale green, plus five interconnecting dining rooms. Furnished only with antiques, these rooms have delicate lace curtains, timbered ceilings, and an array of pictures on their white walls. Our visit coincided with Sunday lunch, and every table was immaculately laid with a white cloth, fine china and gleaming silver; an open fire crackled in the hearth.

The ingredients used in the cooking are mainly produced on the farm. Signora Renzia, a highly regarded chef, travels from Treviso three days a week to produce her exemplary versions of *risotto* and *funghi, porcini e verdura*, while Signora Calzavara cooks a full American breakfast and other meals when required.

The six bedrooms are enchanting. Floors are strewn with rugs; most have wrought-iron bedheads and fine walnut furniture. It's best to book by fax unless you speak Italian.

Nearby Palladian villas; Venice (20 km); Padua (26 km).

Via Marco Polo 2, Levada di
Piombino Dese, Padova
Tel (049) 9350308
Fax (049) 9350016
Location 20 km N of Venice, in
Levada take Via G. Carducci
opposite the church and turn
left into Via Marco Polo; in own
garden with ample parking
Meals breakfast, lunch, dinner
Prices rooms L95,000–
L160,000; standard double
L95,000; breakfast included;
dinner from L45,000

Rooms 6; 4 double and twin, 2
family rooms, all with shower;
all rooms have TV
Facilities dining rooms, sitting
area, garden
Credit cards not accepted
Children accepted, if well-
behaved
Disabled access difficult
Pets not accepted
Closed Jan, Aug
Proprietors Calzavara family

Veneto

Villa Margherita

Another country villa in the Venetian hinterland, this time on the Brenta Riviera, overlooking a flat, industrial landscape but offering peace, seclusion and acres of real estate for your money, while being well placed for excursions into Venice.

Villa Margherita was built in the 17thC as a nobleman's country retreat, and has been open as a hotel since 1987. It is less imposing outside than some of its rival villa-hotels, but attractively furnished within, particularly in the public areas. The yellow and blue breakfast room is gloriously light, with French windows on to the garden, while the sitting room has murals (the principal one portrays a bevy of naked nymphs cavorting on the banks of the Brenta), an open fireplace and some beautiful lamps, vases and antique clocks. Bedrooms are more pedestrian, but thoroughly comfortable; the best lead on to the breakfast terrace.

The Dal Corso family is the driving force behind the hotel and its highly regarded restaurant, 200 metres away across a terrifying road. A lively place, buzzing with locals as well as hotel guests, it specializes in mouthwatering seafood.

Nearby Venice (10 km); Padua (20 km).

Via Nazionale 416–417, 30030 Mira, Venezia
Tel (041) 4265800
Fax (041) 4265838
Location on banks of Brenta river at Mira Porte at the E end of Mira, 10 km W of Venice; in own grounds with ample parking
Meals breakfast, lunch, dinner
Prices rooms L140,000–L275,000; standard double L275,000; breakfast included; menus from L45,000

Rooms 19; 18 double and twin, 3 with bath, 15 with shower; 1 single with shower; all rooms have phone, TV, air-conditioning, minibar, hairdrier **Facilities** breakfast room, sitting room, bar, restaurant (200 m walk), garden, jogging track
Credit cards AE, DC, MC, V
Children accepted **Disabled** several rooms on ground floor
Pets accepted **Closed** never
Proprietors Dal Corso family

Veneto

Agriturismo, Modolo

Fulcio Miari Fulcis

The *raison d'être* of the little hamlet of Modolo is the beautiful 16thC Villa Miari, quite a surprising find in this rural backwater. Nearby is the home of Fulcio Miari Fulcis, nephew of the present owner of Villa Miari, his charming Milanese wife and their young children. And this is very much a *home;* in winter wood is piled up outside, in summer brightly coloured bedclothes hang out of the window to air; children and family pets potter about. There is a pinball machine and a barbecue area. Fulcio is a ski instructor at nearby Nevegàl and also keeps horses, organizing riding expeditions for his guests.

The handsome, green-shuttered farmhouse is typical of the area with the main two-storey building abutting a broad three-storey tower: this wing is reserved for guests. Bedrooms are homely and charming, with a profusion of armchairs and ottomans and an assortment of gaily patterned fabrics. You have a one-in-six chance of occupying a huge hand-carved four-poster from Thailand. Large wood-framed windows give views of the rising hills, and there are rustic beamed ceilings, wooden floors and old doors.

Nearby Belluno (7 km); Nevegàl ski area (10 km).

Località Modolo, 32124 Castion, Belluno
Tel (0437) 927198
Fax (0437) 927198
Location from Belluno, follow signs for Nevegàl; after Castion, turn left signposted Modolo; the house is on the right
Meals breakfast
Prices single L40,000; double L80,000; breakfast included
Rooms 6; 4 double and twin, 2 family; 3 communal bathrooms
Facilities breakfast room, sitting room, sauna, barbecue, garden, horse-riding
Credit cards not accepted
Children welcome
Disabled not suitable
Pets accepted
Closed never
Proprietor Fulcio Miari Fulcis

Veneto

Country villa, Ospedaletto di Pescantina

Villa Quaranta

Ospedaletto earned its name as a stopping-off point on the way to and from the Brenner pass; the 13thC Chapel of Santa Maria di Mezza Campagna, with its Ligozzi frescoes, was where travellers put up. This now forms one side of the Villa Quaranta's pretty inner courtyard: the remainder of the buildings are 17thC. Yet though the hotel's setting, in lovely grounds, is impressive, and its main building imposing, the atmosphere is one of quiet informality. In the restaurant, for example, you are confronted by a vast stone staircase, awe-inspiring frescoed walls, stone-arched doors and tiled floors; yet the ambience is relaxed and the food good value.

Since we last wrote about the hotel for our all-Italy guide, considerable changes have taken place. Bedrooms have proliferated; new ones are spacious, if uniform, with luxury bathrooms, tasteful reproduction furniture, brass fittings, deep-pile carpets. There's a piano bar, pool, terrace bar ... and across the park a luxurious beauty and fitness centre ... and a disco. This last caused a blot on our otherwise happy stay as the roar of revellers' engines continued into the small hours.

Nearby Verona (minibus to opera); Lake Garda (12 km).

Via Brennero, 37026 Ospedaletto di Pescantina, Verona
Tel (045) 6767300
Fax (045) 6767301
Location on SS12, 15 km NW of Verona, in own park with ample parking
Meals breakfast, lunch, dinner
Prices rooms L155,000–L380,000; standard double L230,000–L300,000; breakfast included; dinner from L60,000
Rooms 70; 59 single, double and twin, 11 suites, all with bath; all rooms have phone, TV, air-conditioning, minibar, hairdrier **Facilities** sitting room, dining rooms, bar, TV room, swimming pool, 2 tennis courts (1 indoor), fitness/beauty centre, meeting centre, park with lake **Credit cards** AE, DC, MC, V **Children** accepted
Disabled access possible
Pets not accepted **Closed** hotel never; restaurant Mon
Manager Michel Trüb

Veneto

Villa del Quar

Situated in the fertile Valpolicella valley, this 'typical patrician dwelling' has for the past six years been a luxury hotel, a member of Relais et Châteaux. The ebullient owner and her family live in the fine main villa, while her hotel occupies the east wing. Public rooms in particular make a great impression. The galleried sitting room, an enclosed arcade with beamed roof, is delightfully light, airy and sophisticated. The two dining rooms – resplendent with mirrors, Venetian torches, vast Murano glass chandelier, cream silk tablecloths and elegant dining chairs – are also extremely attractive and make delightful rooms in which to eat. Bedrooms are more restrained, masculine even, many with lovely old cupboard doors. Bathrooms feel luxurious, swathed in prettily coloured marble. If you take a suite, ask for the one with its own terrace, which is no more expensive.

In summer a white awning covers the terrace and the immaculate pool sparkles invitingly. Unfortunately, the villa's setting, though quiet, is not so idyllic; though it is surrounded by a sea of vines, the road is close by and there is a modern housing development on the nearest hillside.

Nearby Verona (11 km); Lake Garda (20 km).

Via Quar 12,
37020 Pedemonte, Verona
Tel (045) 6800681
Fax (045) 6800604
Location in Pedemonte follow signs for Verona and hotel at traffic lights; after about 1,500 m turn right for hotel; in own grounds with ample parking
Meals breakfast, lunch, dinner
Prices rooms L380,000–L600,000; standard double L380,000–L430,000; breakfast included; dinner from L65,000

Rooms 32; 29 double and twin, 3 suites, all with bath; all rooms have phone, TV, air-conditioning, minibar, hairdrier, safe **Facilities** sitting room, 2 dining rooms, breakfast room, bar, terrace, swimming pool, small gym, meeting room **Credit cards** AE, DC, MC, V **Children** accepted **Disabled** rooms on ground floor **Pets** accepted **Closed** Jan to Mar **Proprietor** Evelina Acampora Montresor

Veneto

Restaurant-with-rooms, Pieve d'Alpago

Dolada

A twisting road leads from the Alpago valley to Pieve, and then corkscrews on up to the little hamlet of Plois. Dolada turns out to be a handsome turn-of-the-century building with faded apricot walls and green-shuttered windows with a little garden which looks out over snow-capped mountains and the Santa Croce lake and valley far below. Our inspector reports that although the food was well worth the trip from Belluno, he was glad to be staying the night and not negotiating the hairpin bends after dinner 'although the bright pink of our modern bedroom was a bit of a shocker after our delicious meal in the more sophisticated and mellow surroundings of the dining room'. Each room is themed in a different colour, which can cause a mild feeling of panic if the colour grates.

The point of Dolada is its restaurant, Michelin-starred, which deftly mixes traditional Italian dishes with inventive new ones, and offers a very good wine list. In a series of rooms, lace-clothed tables are set with silver cutlery, with ribbed aluminium lamps suspended over each. Chef Enzo De Pra and his wife Rossanna are very friendly.

Nearby Belluno (20 km); Nevegàl ski area (18 km).

Via Dolada 21, 32010 Plois in Pieve d'Alpago, Belluno
Tel (0437) 479141
Fax (0437) 478068
Location in the hamlet of Plois, signposted from Pieve d'Alpago; ample parking
Meals breakfast, lunch, dinner
Prices rooms L155,000; half board L140,000 per person; breakfast L15,000–L25,000; dinner from L50,000
Rooms 7 double and twin, all with shower; all rooms have phone, TV
Facilities dining room, terrace, garden
Credit cards AE, DC, MC, V
Children accepted
Disabled access difficult to bedrooms
Pets accepted
Closed Jan to Feb; restaurant closed Mon and Tues lunch except July and Aug
Proprietors Enzo and Rossanna De Pra

Veneto

Relais El Toulà

It is difficult to refrain from quoting from the *Alberghi in Ville Venete* brochure about the creation of El Toulà: in 1972, the owner of the 19thC villa, Count Giorgio Guarnieri, entrusted it to hoteliers Alfredo Beltrame and Arturo Filippini. "Create a hotel for me," he apparently said, "where I can live with cheerful people and can see gentlemen with their beautiful lovers, happy couples with well-mannered children, businessmen not wheeler-dealers, a few poets, some generals, admirals or ambassadors." Yes, well. On our visit there was a private party, definitely not admirals or ambassadors, eating lunch to the strains of an electric organ ...

El Toulà is a small luxury hotel with a well-regarded restaurant and a noted wine list. Bedrooms vary from extremely comfortable to extremely luxurious. The two-storey villa, flanked by arcaded wings, is approached by an avenue which is completely covered with red Rubosa vines; at the rear, a wide, rather municipal terrace borders a huge expanse of lawn, fringed by trees; to one side a kidney-shaped pool provides a splash of vivid colour.

Nearby Palladian villas; Treviso (6 km); Venice (40 km).

Via Postumia 63, 31050 Ponzano Veneto, Treviso
Tel (0422) 440751
Fax (0422) 440754
Location 6 km NW of Treviso on Via Postumia between Postioma and Villorba; in own grounds with ample parking
Meals breakfast, lunch, dinner
Prices rooms L230,000–L650,000; double L340,000–L430,000; breakfast L25,000; dinner from L80,000
Rooms 10; 8 double and twin, 2 suites, all with bath; all rooms have phone, TV, air-conditioning, minibar, hairdrier, safe
Credit cards AE, DC, MC, V
Children accepted if well-mannered
Disabled access to ground floor possible, bedrooms difficult
Pets accepted
Closed never
Manager Giorgio Zamuner

Veneto

Villa Giustinian

A solid rectangular white pile with two chimneys stuck incongruously on top like candles on a birthday cake, this villa is surrounded by a park of green lawns filled with statues and
enclosed by a high hedge, which cuts it off from the outside
world. Rooms are of awesome dimensions: hardly intimate, but
certainly impressive. There are several public rooms in pale pas-
tels with newly restored plaster moulding and frescoes, but
nowhere cosy to sit; nevertheless, the atmosphere is pleasantly
unstuffy. A balustraded stairway leads to an immense gallery,
frescoed from floor to ceiling.

There are eight suites in the main villa, usually used for business purposes (several have their own meeting rooms). Two
have extremely elaborate original plasterwork: in one the bed is
enveloped in an over-the-top canopy of draped figures, cherubs
and garlands. Easier to live with are the simpler rooms in the
old stable block, with beams, pretty fabrics and decent reproduction furniture. In the same block are the restaurant, a stylish
setting for excellent fish, and the *enoteca*, where you can sample
a fine collection of wines and eat a snack.
Nearby Pordenone (15 km); Treviso (37 km); Venice (55 km).

Via Giustiniani 11, 31019
Portobuffolé, Treviso
Tel (0422) 850244 **Fax** (0422)
850260 **Location** 9 km N of
Oderzo, in own grounds with
ample parking **Meals** breakfast,
lunch, dinner **Prices** rooms
L120,000–L500,000; standard
double L220,000; breakfast
L15,000; dinner from L70,000
Rooms 43; 28 double and twin,
1 with bath, 27 with shower; 7
single with shower; 8 suites with
bath or shower; all rooms have
phone, TV, fax/modem (on
request), air-conditioning,
minibar, hairdrier, safe
Facilities breakfast/sitting and
conference rooms, bar,
restaurant, *enoteca*, terrace,
garden **Credit cards** AE, DC,
MC, V **Children** accepted
Disabled no special facilities
Pets not accepted **Closed**
restaurant Sun dinner, Mon,
Aug **Proprietors** Berto family

Veneto

Relais Villabella

Don't be put off by the hideous sign set into the portico which spoils an otherwise handsome terracotta frontage. Inside, the Relais Villabella lives up to its name. Built as a humble rice mill and retaining its stone floors and timbered ceilings, it has been cleverly converted to a sophisticated hotel with numerous elegant public rooms and just nine equally elegant bedrooms. Two dining rooms testify to the importance placed on food. The smaller is a refined room, furnished in green, with an open hearth and intimate atmosphere, often used for private dinners. The more formal main restaurant has floor-to-ceiling windows looking on to the garden. The emphasis of the excellent menu is on regional dishes – pasta, risotto, polenta. In a very different style, the piano bar has clusters of shiny black cane tables and chairs around a dance floor, where convention delegates and divas from the Verona opera may smooch the night away.

Bedrooms lead off mysterious, dimly-lit corridors, which might be romantic if you weren't in constant danger of tripping. Some rooms shimmer with mirrored walls and metres of gold and green shot silk fabric; all have luxurious marble bathrooms.
Nearby Vicenza (30 km); Verona (20 km); Palladian villas.

Località Villabella, 37047 San Bonifacio, Verona
Tel (045) 610777
Fax (045) 610799
Location take Castello exit from Soave motorway or sign for Cavalca from SS11, after Sotto Portico, hotel is on the left
Meals breakfast, lunch, dinner
Prices rooms L245,000–L285,000; standard double L245,000; breakfast included; dinner from L60,000
Rooms 9 double and twin, all with bath; all rooms have phone, TV, air-conditioning, minibar, hairdrier
Facilities sitting area, dining rooms, piano bar, meeting room, garden
Credit cards AE, MC, V
Children accepted, if well-behaved
Disabled not suitable
Pets accepted
Closed restaurant Sun, Mon; piano bar Mon
Proprietor Mario Cherubin

Veneto

Locanda San Vigilio

In general the east side of Lake Garda is less upmarket than the west but this hotel's idyllic setting, on a lush peninsula dotted with olive trees and cypresses, is a conspicuous exception. The property is owned by Conte Agostino Guarienti, who lives in the 16thC villa that dominates the headland. An air of discreet exclusivity pervades the *locanda* (royalty are among regular guests) yet the atmosphere is far from stuffy. Of the public rooms, our favourite is the elegant dining room, right on the lake, with a comfortingly creaky wooden floor. A ceramic stove occupies one corner and sideboards display plates and bottles. You can eat in here, on a little arched veranda or under huge white umbrellas on the terrace where terracotta pots overflow with flowers. Next door is a cosy sitting room.

The seven bedrooms in the main house are all different, though they have beautiful antiques and fabrics in common. Only one has no view. Other bedrooms are in separate buildings and more rustic in style. In the evening the place comes into its own: with the day trippers gone, guests can wander the peninsula or sit with a drink at one of the Taverna's vine-shaded tables.
Nearby Garda (2 km); Verona (45 km); ferry services (4 km).

San Vigilio, 37016 Garda, Verona
Tel (045) 7256688
Fax (045) 7256551
Location 2 km W of Garda, on promontory; parking available 150 m away
Meals breakfast, lunch, dinner
Prices rooms L300,000–L960,000; standard double L400,000–L480,000; breakfast included; dinner from L45,000
Rooms 14; 11 double and twin, 3 suites, all with bath or shower; all rooms have phone, TV, air-conditioning, minibar, hairdrier; most rooms have safe
Facilities sitting room, dining room, bar, terrace, walled garden
Credit cards AE, DC, MC, V
Children accepted, if well-behaved
Disabled not suitable
Pets accepted **Closed** Nov to just before Easter
Proprietor Conte Agostino Guarienti

Veneto

Villa Conestabile

Standing at the centre of the hard-working town of Scorzè, this aristocratic villa dates back to the 16thC, but was remodelled in the 18thC in elegant neoclassical style. Visible from its earliest period (especially if you take room No. 1) are fragments of gorgeous School of Veronese frescoes. There are also fine ceilings and floors, an impressive double staircase and a park modelled in the early 19thC in Romantic English style. The spacious first-floor rooms are somewhat staid but full of character, recalling the last century when they were the bedrooms of the noble Conestabile family, retaining their lofty proportions, and, in some cases, original faux marble walls. Rooms on the second floor, formerly the household quarters, are plainer but spacious and furnished in different styles.

On her March visit our inspector reports that she ate alone in the dining room, but was comforted by the familial ambience, with copper pans hanging from the ceiling and old dressers laden with wine bottles, and by a simple but well-prepared set menu. She also notes that her visit was marred by one of the coolest welcomes in reception that she can remember.

Nearby Riviera del Brenta; Venice (24 km); Padua (30 km).

Via Roma 1, 30037 Scorzè, Venezia
Tel (041) 445027
Fax (041) 5840088
Location in Scorzè, 24 km NW of Venice, in own grounds with ample parking
Meals breakfast, lunch, dinner
Prices rooms L110,000–L200,000; first floor double rooms L200,000; second floor double rooms L160,000; breakfast included; dinner L39,000

Rooms 22; 19 double and twin, 3 single, 16 with shower, 6 with bath; all rooms have phone, TV
Facilities sitting room, dining room, bar, breakfast room, meeting room, terrace, garden
Credit cards AE, DC, MC, V
Children accepted
Disabled not suitable
Pets accepted
Closed hotel never; restaurant closed Sun, Jan, Feb, Nov, 2 weeks in Aug
Proprietors Martinelli family

Veneto

Locanda da Lino

The creation of an inspired chef, Lino Toffolin, this restaurant has become an institution. Championed by the diva Toti Dal Monte, the young Lino was soon cooking for the *glitterati* and being patronized by stars such as Marcello Mastroianni. Now run by Lino's family, the restaurant seems to have lost none of its verve. One long room, with smaller rooms leading off it, can seat 400 for dinner at full stretch. The ceilings are hung with hundreds of copper pots. A table in the 'inner sanctum' enables you to glimpse food being grilled over a blazing furnace. From a menu of local delicacies, we particularly enjoyed *antipasto misto della Locanda, braciole di vitello ai ferri* and *polpettine in umido con polenta*, and there's an impressive wine list from the beautifully laid-out cellar.

The bedrooms are in annexes and range from comfortable doubles to the extravagantly rococo Elsa Vazzoler suite with its bright blue walls, enormous gilt lamps, and cherubs above the bed. The L-shaped entrance/bar/breakfast area is also furnished with rococo pieces, mixed eclectically but successfully with modern art. If you can't stay here, at least try to come for a meal.
Nearby Palladian villas; Asolo (20 km).

Via Brandolini 31, 31050 Solighetto, Treviso
Tel (0438) 82150/842377
Fax (0438) 980577
Location in Solighetto on the Follina road; with ample parking
Meals breakfast, lunch, dinner
Prices rooms L90,000–L160,000; standard double L110,000; breakfast L15,000; dinner from L45,000
Rooms 17; 10 double and twin, 7 suites, all with bath; all rooms have phone, TV, minibar, hairdrier
Facilities breakfast area/bar, restaurant, terrace
Credit cards AE, DC, MC, V
Children accepted
Disabled several rooms on ground floor
Pets accepted
Closed restaurant Mon, Christmas Day, July
Proprietors 'Lino' family

Veneto

Gardesana

Torri del Benaco is one of the showpiece fishing villages which are dotted along the shore of Lake Garda, and Gardesana is in a plum position. It is a treat to tuck into the chef's speciality fish soup on the delightful first-floor dining terrace which overlooks the central *piazza*, 14thC castle and bustling port. The wrought-iron balustrade is decked with cascading geraniums, the tables are elegant, the waiters smartly uniformed, and the food, particularly the fish, fresh and delicious. It makes a perfect vantage point for watching the boats come and go, and the changing colours of the lake. Drinks can also be taken on the ground-floor terrace, which extends out on to the *piazza*.

The building has a long history, as its exterior would suggest, with its stone arches and mellow stucco walls; but the entire interior has been smartly modernized in recent years to produce an essentially modern and very comfortable hotel. The green and white bedrooms are almost all identical: wooden furnishings, soft fabrics, plenty of little extras. If you can, try to book one of the corner rooms; these have the advantage of facing both the lake and the *piazza*.

Nearby Bardolino (11 km); Malcensine (21 km).

Piazza Calderini 20, 37010
Torri del Benaco, Verona
Tel (045) 7225411
Fax (045) 7225771
Location in town centre, on waterfront, in pedestrian zone; unload at hotel, private parking 150 m away
Meals breakfast, lunch, dinner
Prices rooms L85,000–L200,000; standard double L130,000–L170,000; breakfast included; dinner from L50,000
Facilities dining room, bar, lift, terrace
Credit cards AE, DC, MC, V
Children accepted
Disabled no special facilities
Pets not accepted
Closed Nov and Dec
Proprietor Giuseppe Lorenzini

Veneto

Restaurant-with-rooms, Trissino

Relais Ca' Masieri

The countryside around industrial Arzignano is uninspiring, but things improve as you wind your way to Masieri through willow-fringed meadows. Through wrought-iron gates and at the end of a long drive, the sight of Ca' Masieri itself, a fine old shuttered mansion with swimming pool and shady terrace further lifts the spirits. In our case, they were immediately cast down, because we were late and the chef had just gone home: we had been dreaming of the much-vaunted food all morning. The sight of the charming little restaurant, its walls decorated with delicate 18thC frescoes, only made our disappointment worse. Had we been in time, we might have had the salad of crayfish tails followed by risotto with herbs, and then the casserole of pigeon ...

The bedrooms are in an adjacent building which retains its old wooden beamed ceilings, but is otherwise furnished in contemporary style. Two rooms have spiral metal staircases from a sitting area up to the mezzanine beds. No. 201 is huge, with a terrace overlooking the hills and Trissino. There are pretty bedspreads in William Morris leaf-print, curvy modern tables, and stylish bathrooms with walls painted the colour of aluminium. **Nearby** Vicenza (21 km); Verona (49 km).

Località Masieri, Via Masieri, 36070 Trissino, Vicenza
Tel (0445) 490122
Fax (0445) 490455
Location from Trissino, follow signs to Masieri, and in Via Masieri to Ca' Masieri up a private drive; ample parking
Meals breakfast, lunch, dinner
Prices rooms L100,000–L190,000; standard double L145,000; breakfast L12,000; dinner from L60,000
Rooms 8; 3 double, 3 single, 2 family, all with shower; all rooms have phone, TV, minibar; 4 have air-conditioning
Facilities sitting room, bar, breakfast room, dining room, terrace, swimming pool
Credit cards AE, MC, V
Children accepted
Disabled not suitable
Pets accepted
Closed late Jan to mid-Feb
Proprietor Angelo Vassena

Veneto

Town hotel, Verona

Colomba d'Oro

The hotel stands opposite the friendly little Torcolo (see page 90) which, though simple, is much more in the spirit of our guide. Nevertheless, the smart, slick Colomba d'Oro should not be ignored, if for no other reason than its eye-catching lobby, muralled with consummate skill by a young artist in 1996. Three months and two assistants later, the result was a charming evocation of Renaissance Verona, with faux marble pillars and statues, balcony scenes on the ceiling and dreamy vistas of lakes, rivers and Roman ruins on the walls.

A hotel since 1880, the Tapparini family have been in charge since 1927 and have engaged in constant refurbishment over the years. Today, it is in excellent condition; bedrooms are *à la mode*, some with water-silk fabric on the walls and matching bedspreads, others in glossy modern style, with gleaming *spatolato* walls in golden yellow, pale green or deep pink, and polished wood fittings. Despite the romantic foyer, a fairly impersonal, business-oriented air pervades, especially in the breakfast room and the large sitting room, with its abundance of formal leather seating.

Nearby Arena; Via Mazzini, Piazza delle Erbe.

Via Cattaneo 10, 37121 Verona
Tel (045) 595300
Fax (045) 594974
Location in city centre, just off Piazza Brà; parking in hotel garage or public car park in Piazza Cittadella
Meals breakfast
Prices rooms L180,000–L372,000; standard double L260,000–L310,000; breakfast included
Rooms 51; 26 double and twin, 15 single, 10 junior suites; 39 rooms with bath, 12 with shower; all rooms have phone, TV, air-conditioning, minibar, hairdrier
Facilities sitting room, breakfast room, bar, meeting room, lift
Credit cards AE, DC, MC, V
Children accepted
Disabled access difficult
Pets accepted
Closed never
Proprietor Alberto Tapparini

Veneto

Town hotel, Verona

Gabbia d'Oro

This stylish hotel in a 17thC *palazzo*, luxurious but never ostentatious, boasts an attention to detail rarely encountered nowadays. A small, beautifully wrapped gift awaits your arrival, and the staff are as charming and polished as the hotel itself. The public rooms, entered through massive wood doors with gilt decoration, are comfortable as well as elegant: there are plenty of places in which to sit and relax, and sofas are large and deep. Wooden floors, beams and brickwork are much in evidence; the sitting room shares one wall with the Gardello Tower. Furnishings, chandeliers, silver-framed photographs, ornaments and antiques are always in keeping. Little lamps lend a glow to the panelled bar, and the new orangery is restful, with its green and white colour scheme and view to the terrace.

Frescoes, restored or reproduced from the originals, recur as friezes both downstairs and in the bedrooms. Suites outnumber doubles. In almost all, beds are shrouded in a canopy of antique lace. No. 404, dark red with sloping walls, rafters, and nooks and crannies, is so romantic that it's normally chosen for honeymooners. Prices are high, but we felt justifiably so.
Nearby Piazza delle Erbe; Loggia del Consiglio; Arena.

Corso Portoni Borsari 4a,
37121 Verona
Tel (045) 8003060
Fax (045) 590293
Location in medieval centre of the city, S of Porta Borsari; garage parking available
Meals breakfast
Prices rooms L250,000–L1,200,000; standard double L250,000–L550,000; breakfast L45,000
Rooms 27; 8 double and twin, 19 suites, all with bath or shower; all rooms have phone, TV, air-conditioning, minibar, hairdrier, safe
Facilities breakfast room, sitting room, orangery, bar, meeting room, lift, terrace
Credit cards AE, DC, MC, V
Children accepted
Disabled access difficult
Pets accepted
Closed never
Proprietor Signora Balzarro

Veneto

Town hotel, Verona

Torcolo

The Torcolo is an inexpensive hotel in an excellent location at the heart of lively Verona. 'Its most outstanding quality,' writes one recent guest, 'was the warmth and friendliness of our welcome and the consistent helpfulness of the staff'. Every room is individually decorated in varying styles – Italian 18thC, art nouveau, modern – and all are fresher and have more charm than one normally finds at this price. Ours contained a complete set of Liberty-style bedroom furniture which had belonged to owner Silvia Pommari's parents when they first married. It was set off by white linen curtains and a colourful patchwork bedspread. Ceramic tiled bathrooms are somewhat cramped; the best have separate shower cubicles. Rooms are double-glazed against the considerable street sounds (people, not cars) but, despite air-conditioning, they can get fuggy, especially in warm weather. Breakfast, including a jug of fresh juice, a good assortment of bread and croissants and yoghurt, can be taken in your room, which might be preferable to the cramped little breakfast room. In summer, it is served buffet-style in the small off-street courtyard.
Nearby Arena; Via Mazzini, Piazza delle Erbe.

Vicolo Listone 3, 37121 Verona
Tel (045) 8007512
Fax (045) 8004058
Location just off Piazza Brà; park in public car park in Piazza Cittadella
Meals breakfast
Prices rooms L80,000–L135,000; standard double L110,000–L135,000; breakfast L10,000–L15,000
Rooms 17 double, twin and single, 2 family, one with bath and 18 with shower; all rooms have phone, TV, air-conditioning, hairdrier; 10 rooms have minibar and safe
Facilities sitting area, breakfast room, courtyard, lift
Credit cards AE, MC, V
Children accepted
Closed 10–31 Jan
Disabled access difficult
Pets accepted
Proprietors Silvia Pommari and Diana Castellani

Veneto

Country villa, Zerman di Mogliano Veneto

Villa Condulmer

For the price of a three star in San Marco you can stay in this impressive 18thC villa a 20-minute drive away. Flanked by low annexes, it stands four-square in a miniature park landscaped by Sebatoni. From the moment we walked in we were struck by the sheer scale not only of the rooms, but the furnishings. The vast central hall is decorated with baroque stucco in different hues, inset with murals. Two extravagantly large Murano chandeliers hang from the high ceiling, but armchairs make it a room to sit in, not just admire. A pair of grand pianos bear witness to Verdi's visits here. The more dilapidated is his; the other, a copy. The menu in the restful pale green and white dining room verges on the pretentious, but don't pass up a drink in the intimate stuccoed bar.

The most exotic – and expensive – bedrooms are the upstairs suites (Ronald Reagan slept in No. 4). The double rooms in the main villa have been redecorated using bright silk damasks, but we preferred the more restrained annexe rooms, where the peace and quiet, the comfortable beds and the heavenly linen sheets should guarantee a good night's sleep.
Nearby Palladian villas; Venice (18 km).

Via Zermanese 1, 31020 Zerman di Mogliano Veneto, Treviso
Tel (041) 457100
Fax (041) 457134
Location 12 km S of Treviso, N of road to Mogliano Veneto; in own grounds with ample parking
Meals breakfast, lunch, dinner
Prices rooms L190,000–L400,000; standard double L280,000; breakfast included; menus from L70,000 **Rooms** 48 double and twin, single, junior suites, 2 apartments, all with bath or shower; all rooms have phone, TV, air-conditioning, minibar, hairdrier **Facilities** breakfast room, bar, sitting rooms, meeting room, TV room, dining rooms, garden, swimming pool, tennis courts
Credit cards AE, DC, MC, V
Children accepted
Disabled access difficult
Pets accepted **Closed** never
Proprietor Davide Zuin

Lombardia

Lakeside restaurant-with-rooms, Gardone Riviera

Villa Fiordaliso

Michelin-starred Villa Fiordaliso has been well-known as one of the best restaurants in Northern Italy for some years, but it is also a chic and romantic small hotel. Built in 1902, the pale pink and white lakeside villa was home to Gabriele d'Annunzio, and later to Claretta Petacci, Mussolini's mistress. Inside, the intricately carved wood and marble work on walls, floors and doorways and the splendid gold and frescoed ceilings are the perfectly preserved remnants of another age. A magnificent Venetian-style marble staircase, with columns and delicate wrought ironwork leads from the reception hall at garden level to the intimate first-floor restaurant and up to the seven luxurious bedrooms. Three of these have been left with their original furniture and decoration. The Claretta suite, a room of impressive dimensions with terrace and lake view, has a stunning marble bathroom. Other rooms are lighter in style with fresh wallpapers and fabrics.

The shady garden, bordering the lake (and, unfortunately, the main road), is a wonderful setting for the elegant summer restaurant, immaculately decked out in a terracotta and white colour scheme.

Nearby Brescia (40 km); Sirmione (35 km).

Via Zanardelli 150, 25083
Gardone Riviera, Brescia
Tel (0365) 20158
Fax (0365) 290011
Location on SS572, 3 km NE of Salò; in grounds with ample parking
Meals breakfast, lunch, dinner
Prices rooms L300,000–L700,000; standard double L300,000; breakfast included; dinner from L75,000
Rooms 7; 5 double, 2 suites, all with bath or shower; all rooms have phone, TV, air-conditioning, minibar
Facilities dining room, sitting room, tower with bar, terraces, garden
Credit cards AE, DC, MC, V
Children accepted, but not suitable
Disabled access to restaurant possible
Pets not accepted
Closed Jan to mid-Mar; restaurant Mon, Tues lunch
Proprietors Tosetti family

Lombardia

Villa del Sogno

Built in 1904 as the holiday home of an Austrian silk industrial-
ist, this imposing villa became a hotel in 1938. Like so many of
the hotels around Lake Garda, it has an amazing position, above
the lake but near enough to feel part of the lakeside scene. It is
approached by a long winding drive and cradled in exotic gardens, where we stumbled upon two little neoclassical temples. An
extension added in the 1980s contains some rather ordinary
rooms, including the reception (disappointing when you first
arrive). But go through to the wood-panelled hall and staircase
and you'll find much more character. The huge wooden fireplace and painted ceramic tiles reveal the villa's Austrian her-
itage, which is only slightly at odds with the stone arches,
Grecian urns, and other neoclassical flourishes.

Armchairs in cheerful floral prints and a bar at one end make
the sitting room especially congenial. There is also a refined
restaurant in two rooms, where the parquet floor gleams almost
as much as the silver candlesticks. Upstairs, there are several
enormous suites, furnished traditionally. Rooms in the new wing
are lighter with their own terraces.

Nearby beach (300 m); Brescia (50 km).

Via Zanardelli 107, 25083
Gardone Riviera, Brescia
Tel (0365) 290181
Fax (0365) 290230
Location 2 km N of Gardone,
off the SS45; in own grounds
with ample parking
Meals breakfast, lunch, dinner
Prices rooms L200,000–
L560,000; standard double
L320,000–L480,000; breakfast
included; dinner from L90,000
Rooms 32; 25 double and twin,
20 with bath, 5 with shower; 7
suites with bath; all rooms have
phone, TV, hairdrier; 9 have
air-conditioning
Facilities sitting room/bar,
dining room, sauna, solarium,
lift, terrace, garden, swimming
pool, tennis courts
Credit cards AE, DC, MC, V
Children accepted
Disabled no special facilities
Pets accepted
Closed mid-Oct to end Mar (or
Easter if earlier)
Proprietors Caldaran family

Lombardia

Baia d'Oro

Giambattista Terzi was born in one of a pair of neighbouring fishermen's cottages built on the edge of the lake in 1780, and his wife was the moving force behind turning them into a hotel in the 1960s. Since then the facilities have slowly been updated. To appreciate the fabulous setting, you should arrive by boat.

You can almost dip your hand in the lake from the romantic dining terrace, a splendid vantage point from which to watch night succeed day to the gentle lapping of the water. Boats dock at a little jetty also used by sunbathers. For cool nights, there's a pleasant dining room overlooking the terrace to the lake. Here Terzi's son Gabriele is in charge, and the fine, short menu consists of saltwater and freshwater fish, served simply.

The Terzis are gradually redecorating the bedrooms in slightly dubious shades of pink and blue, with painted wooden furniture, shiny fabrics and mirrored glass bedheads. Not to everyone's taste, but they are comfortable with sparkling new bathrooms, and the doubles all have lake views.

The cosy, low-ceilinged sitting room has an open fire, and Giambattista's paintings of the area cover the walls.

Nearby Gardone Riviera (12 km); Sirmione (48 km).

Via Gamberera 13, 25084 Gargnano, Brescia
Tel (0365) 71171/72078
Fax (0365) 72568
Location on edge of town, on lake; with private parking
Meals breakfast, lunch, dinner
Prices rooms L130,000–L220,000; standard double L220,000; breakfast included; dinner from L40,000
Rooms 13; 10 double and twin, 2 with bath, 8 with shower; 3 single with shower; 1 suite with bath; all rooms have phone, TV, minibar, hairdrier, safe
Facilities sitting room, dining room, bar, terrace, sun deck
Credit cards not accepted
Children accepted
Disabled not suitable
Pets accepted
Closed mid-Nov to mid-Mar
Proprietors Terzi family

Lombardia

Villa Giulia

From a *pensione* with no private bathrooms, the Giulia has been upgraded over the years to a three-star hotel, and work is now underway to renovate existing rooms and create new suites. Happily, however, this beautiful late-19thC Victorian villa with Gothic touches still retains the atmosphere of a family-run guest house. Rina Bombardelli has been here for 45 years, and has gradually made the Giulia one of the most delightful places to stay on Lake Garda. It has a glorious location, with gardens of lawns and oleanders, running down to a low wall at the water's edge. Only the pool looks a little scruffy.

The villa is painted the palest of pinks with dark brown shutters and woodwork. Inside, airy rooms lead off handsome corridors: a beautiful dining room with Murano chandeliers, gold walls and elegant seats; a civilized sitting room with Victorian armchairs; and bedrooms in a variety of styles: some are light and modern, others are large, with rafters, antiques and balconies. We met one unhappy solo visitor, who claimed that the singles are not nearly as attractive as the doubles. Our favourites are the rooms in the eaves with Gothic windows.

Nearby ferry services.

Viale Rimembranze 20, 25084 Gargnano, Brescia
Tel (0365) 71022/71289
Fax (0365) 72774
Location 150 m from town centre; in own gardens with ample parking
Meals breakfast, lunch, dinner
Prices rooms L120,000– L300,000; standard double L240,000–L260,000; breakfast included; dinner from L60,000
Rooms 27; 20 double and twin, 4 with bath, 16 with shower; 3 single with shower; 4 suites with bath; all rooms have phone, TV, minibar, hairdrier, safe
Facilities sitting room, TV room, dining rooms, sauna, veranda, terrace, garden, swimming pool, beach
Credit cards AE, DC, MC, V
Children accepted
Disabled 2 rooms on ground floor **Pets** accepted
Closed mid-Oct to 1 week before Easter
Proprietors Bombardelli family

Lombardia

Grifone

Although the Grifone is one of the cheapest and simplest hotels in this guide, it also has one of the loveliest locations, and makes a great place to stay for a night or two. Essentially it is a restaurant specializing in fish, with a mouth-watering selection of *antipasto* to start. It has an enticing tree-filled terrace overlooking both Lake Garda and the ramparts of Sirmione's castle; also a tiny sandy beach.

The entrance to the hotel is found off a narrow street just inside the city walls. A small sitting room equipped with television and cheerful bamboo furniture leads to a little patio where breakfast is served, and, if the water beckons, on to the scrap of beach. Upstairs, rooms are simple, furniture is basic, but everything is spotless. Some rooms look right over the castle walls, and the five balconies are full of flowers. Those on the top floor enjoy the best views: rooftops, mountains, and of course the lake. There is no traffic noise in this pedestrian zone, but you may be woken by church bells. The younger generation of the Marcolini family – brother and sister – who now run the Grifone are friendly and helpful.

Nearby Lake Garda; Brescia (39 km); Verona (35 km).

Vicolo Bisse (Via Bocchio) 5, 25019 Sirmione, Brescia
Tel (030) 916014
Fax (030) 916548
Location just inside city walls, next to castle, on lake with free parking (50 m)
Meals breakfast, lunch, dinner
Prices rooms L50,000– L105,000; standard double L78,000; breakfast included
Rooms 16; 12 double, twin and triple, 4 with bath, 8 with shower; 4 single all with shower

Facilities sitting room, dining room, lift, terraces, tiny beach
Credit cards not accepted
Children accepted
Disabled access difficult except to restaurant
Pets accepted
Closed Nov to Easter
Proprietors Marcolini family

Friuli-Venezia Giulia

Converted mill, Bannia di Fiume Veneto

L'Ultimo Mulino

As the name suggests, this 17thC building is one of the very last functioning mills in the area. In use until the 1970s, the three old wooden wheels are still in working condition; indeed, they are set in motion in the evenings for the benefit of guests. The lovely stone house and garden are set in gentle farmland and surrounded by three rivers; the soothing sounds of water are everywhere.

Opened as a hotel in 1994, restoration work has been carried out with great taste and flair, preserving as much as possible of the original character of the house. The long, open-plan sitting room and bar area have even incorporated the hefty innards of the mill machinery. Throughout, attractive Laura Ashley fabrics are teamed with handsome antique furniture, rustic stone and woodwork, and soft, elegant lighting. The comfortable and stylish bedrooms, while different in layout, are all along similar lines with wooden fittings and pale green and cream country fabrics. Those on the second floor have attic ceilings and some have squashy sofas. The sparkling, well-equipped bathrooms are in pale grey marble.

Nearby Pordenone (10 km); Venice (80 km); Trieste (80 km).

Via Molino 45, 33080 Bannia di Fiume Veneto, Pordenone
Tel (0434) 957911
Fax (0434) 958483
Location 10 km SE of Pordenone, exit from A28 at Azzano Decimo; in own garden with parking
Meals breakfast, dinner
Prices rooms L140,000–L180,000; standard double L180,000; breakfast included; dinner L65,000
Rooms 8 double and twin, 4 with bath, 4 with shower; all rooms have phone, TV, air-conditioning, minibar, hairdrier
Facilities breakfast room, sitting rooms, dining rooms, bar, music/conference room, garden, terrace
Credit cards AE, DC, MC, V
Children welcome
Disabled no special facilities
Pets accepted
Closed 10 days Jan, Aug
Proprietors Balestrieri family

Friuli-Venezia Giulia

Country villa, Rivarotta

Villa Luppis

This rambling and mellow L-shaped building, acquired by the
Luppis family in the 1800s, was once a monastery. Set in gentle
countryside, there is not much sign of Spartan living today; it is
now a comfortable and elegant yet relaxed hotel run by Giorgio
Luppis and his wife. One side of the 'L' is a long room incorpo-
rating reception hall, sitting room and bar, bright and welcoming with low, timbered ceiling and central columns. At the front
of the house is the equally long main restaurant – a dreamy
room with pale pink and white table linen, period furniture,
antique silver and fresh flowers. There is (rather incongruously)
also a piano bar with dance floor. Long corridors, softly lit and
thickly carpeted, lead to the luxurious bedrooms which are furnished with period pieces, and have superior king-size beds. Fine
fabrics – Regency stripes or fresh chintzes – are co-ordinated
with soft carpeting, and the suites have separate sitting areas.

The villa's extensive park with its venerable old trees and
green lawns has a pleasant pool and a newly built fitness centre.
A minibus service runs to and from Venice (only 45 minutes
away) every day.

Nearby Pordenone (15 km); Treviso (35 km); Venice (50 km).

Via San Martino 34, 33087
Rivarotta, Pordenone
Tel (0434) 626969
Fax (0434) 626228
Location 15 km S of
Pordenone; exit A4 at Cessalto,
and take road for Motta di
Livenza; in extensive grounds
with ample parking
Meals breakfast, lunch, dinner
Prices rooms L130,000–
L450,000; standard double
L300,000; breakfast included;
dinner from L80,000

Rooms 21; 18 double and twin,
3 suites, all with bath; all rooms
have phone, TV, air-
conditioning, hairdrier
Facilities sitting room, dining
room, bar, meeting room, lift,
terraces, gardens, swimming
pool, tennis court, gym
Credit cards AE, DC, MC, V
Children welcome
Disabled access possible
Pets accepted **Closed** never
Proprietors Giorgio and
Stefania Luppis

Friuli-Venezia Giulia

Converted castle, San Floriano del Collio

Golf Hotel

Unfortunately, this is one of only a handful of hotels which we were unable to inspect personally, although it has long been included in our all-Italy guide. Judging by past reports, however, we are happy to recommend it, but we would welcome some more recent feedback.

The hotel's name, referring to its nine-hole golf course (closed Mon; green fee L30,000), gives the impression of something modern, but it is in fact two ancient renovated houses just outside the walls of Castello Formentini, which has belonged to the Formentini family since the 16thC. The present owner, Contessa Isabella Formentini, has filled the rooms of the tiny hotel with family furniture and pictures. Each beautifully decorated and spacious bedroom is named after a prestigious wine, emphasizing the vinous interest of the Formentini family. Three of them are within the castle walls, but all guests are at liberty to use the castle grounds and its swimming pool. The family also run an excellent restaurant called Castello Formentini (closed Mon, Tues lunch). This is a charming spot, with gentle, wooded countryside spread out around the hilltop castle.
Nearby Gorizia (4 km); Trieste (47 km).

Via Oslavia 2, 34070 San Floriano del Collio, Gorizia
Tel (0481) 884051
Fax (0481) 884052
Location in town, just outside castle walls; private grounds; parking
Meals breakfast
Prices rooms L170,000–L320,000; standard double L300,000; breakfast included
Rooms 15; 12 double and twin, 2 single, 1 suite in tower, all with bath or shower; all rooms have TV, minibar; 12 rooms have phone; 3 rooms have no phone but air-conditioning
Facilities sitting room ,breakfast room, garden, swimming pool, tennis court, nine-hole golf course
Credit cards AE, DC, MC, V
Children accepted
Disabled not suitable
Pets accepted
Closed Dec to Mar
Proprietor Contessa Isabella Formentini

Trentino-Alto Adige

Mountain hotel, Barbiano

Bad Dreikirchen

The name of this idyllically situated hotel derives from its vicinity to the cluster of three small churches which date back to the Middle Ages. The fact that you can only reach the hotel by four-wheel-drive taxi, or by a hearty half-hour hike makes for a perfect escape from the pressures of city life.

The large old building with its shingled roof and dark wood balconies is surrounded by meadows, woods, mountains and fresh air; no traffic noise spoils the peace. There's plenty of space for guests, both inside and out, and the atmosphere is comfortably rustic with an abundance of aromatic pine panelling and carved furniture. A cosy library provides a quiet corner for reading, and excellent meals are served in the pleasant dining room or on the adjacent veranda, from which the views are superb. Bedrooms in the original part of the house are particularly charming, being entirely wood-panelled.

To sum up, the words of one seasoned traveller, a guest at Bad Dreikirchen in 1908, are appropriate: 'I stayed for some days ... the weather was continually fine, the position, dominating the Val d'Isarco, magnificent, and the food good.'

Nearby Bressanone (17 km); Val Gardena (10 km).

San Giacomo 6, 39040 Barbiano, Bolzano
Tel/Fax (0471) 650055
Location 21 km NE of Bolzano, exit from Brennero Autostrada at Chiusa, head S through Barbiano (6 km); hotel car park on right (call and the hotel will send a jeep to collect you from car park)
Meals breakfast, lunch, dinner
Prices half board L64,000–L97,000 per person per day
Rooms 33; 15 double and twin, 15 single, 3 family, most with shower
Facilities sitting rooms, bar, restaurant, games room, library, garden, terraces, swimming pool, tennis court
Credit cards not accepted
Children welcome
Disabled access difficult
Pets accepted
Closed Nov to 1 week before Easter
Proprietors Wodenegg family

Trentino-Alto Adige

Elefant

Bressanone is a pretty town at the foot of the Brenner Pass, more Austrian than Italian in character. The same is true of the charming Elefant, named after a beast which was led over the Alps for Emperor Ferdinand of Austria's amusement. The only stable big enough for the exhausted animal was next to the inn, so the innkeeper promptly changed its name to celebrate the event.

There is an air of solid, old-fashioned comfort throughout. Corridors decorated in sumptuous colours are lined with heavily carved and beautifully inlaid antiques. The public rooms are all on the first floor: an elegant 18thC-style sitting room, a large light breakfast room, and three dining rooms. The main one is panelled in dark wood with a vast green ceramic stove and stags' heads on the walls. The food is one of the highlights of a stay here. A reporter commented recently, 'We had a fabulous dinner; the cooking is imaginative but unfussy with lots of fresh herbs and local ingredients, beautifully presented and bountiful.' Bedrooms are large and comfortable, but disappointing compared with the public areas. Some have antiques, others have none.

Nearby cathedral; Novacella monastery (3 km).

Via Rio Bianco 4, 39042 Bressanone, Bolzano
Tel (0472) 832750
Fax (0472) 836579
Location at N end of town; in gardens with parking and garages
Meals breakfast, lunch, dinner
Prices rooms L124,000–L270,000; standard double L248,000–L270,000; breakfast included; dinner from L48,000
Rooms 44; 28 double and twin, all with bath; 16 single, 15 with bath, one with shower; all rooms have phone, TV, hairdrier
Facilities breakfast room, sitting room, bar, dining rooms, garden, swimming pool, tennis courts
Credit cards AE, DC, MC, V
Children accepted
Disabled 2 ground-floor rooms in annexe **Pets** accepted
Closed Nov to Christmas, Jan to Mar
Proprietor Elizabeth Falk

Trentino-Alto Adige

Leuchtenburg

This solid stone-built 16thC hostel once housed the servants of Leuchtenburg castle, an arduous hour's trek up the steep wooded mountain behind. Today, guests in the *pensione* are well cared for by the friendly young owners, while the castle lies in ruins. The setting is enviably tranquil, right on Lago di Caldaro, better known (at least to wine buffs) as Kalterer See. Cross a narrow road and you are at the water's edge, where a little private beach is dotted with umbrellas and sunloungers.

Back in the *pensione*, the Sparers provide solid breakfasts and three-course dinners of regional cuisine in an unpretentious, homely atmosphere. White-painted low-arched dining rooms occupy the ground floor; above is the reception, with a large table littered with magazines and surrounded by armchairs. There is another sitting area on the first floor, leading to the bedrooms. These have pretty painted furniture and tiled floors (second-floor rooms are plainer). Each one tells a story: for example, the 'old smoke room' was where food was smoked. All the rooms are large, and some share the views enjoyed from the terrace across vineyards to the lake.

Nearby Swimming and fishing in lake.

Campo di Lago 100, 39052 Caldaro, Bolzano
Tel (0471) 960048
Fax (0471) 960093
Location 5 km SE of Caldaro, on the edge of the lake; in courtyard with parking
Meals breakfast, dinner
Prices rooms L40,000–L140,000; standard double L100,000; breakfast included; dinner from L25,000
Rooms 19; 15 double and twin, 3 with bath, 12 with shower; 2 single, 2 triple, all with shower; rooms have TV (on request)
Facilities sitting area, dining area, bar, terrace, beach
Credit cards not accepted
Children accepted
Disabled not suitable
Pets accepted
Closed Nov to Easter
Proprietor Markus Sparer

Trentino-Alto Adige

Town hotel, Castelrotto

Cavallino d'Oro

Records of this establishment, once a coaching inn, date back to 1393. Now a four-star hotel, it manages to retain the ambience of a typical hostelry situated in the heart of the Italian Tyrol. Located on the central square of historic Castelrotto, the hotel's name is reflected in its sign of a golden horse. Inside, it is overflowing with character; the two panelled *stübe*, dating from the 1700s, make charming dining rooms, and public rooms are full of beautifully carved wood furniture, much of it antique and collected by the three generations of Urthalers who have run the hotel. The restaurant is well known for its local cuisine.

Some of the spacious, individually decorated bedrooms are furnished with prettily painted Tyrolean pieces while others have plenty of old pine and marvellous intricately carved four-poster beds. The south-facing rooms all have balconies with superb mountain views. The surrounding area is excellent for cross-country skiing, with a bus service to the nearby Alps of Siusi for downhill enthusiasts.

The energetic hosts, Stefan and Susanne, both speak excellent English.

Nearby Alpe de Siusi; Val Gardena.

Piazza Kraus, 39040 Castelrotto, Bolzano
Tel (0471) 706337
Fax (0471) 707172
Location in town centre, 24 km NE of Bolzano; ample parking
Meals breakfast, lunch, dinner
Prices rooms L122,000–L248,000; standard double L173,000; breakfast included; dinner from L40,000
Rooms 22; 17 double and twin, 2 single, 3 suites, all with bath; all rooms have phone, TV, hairdrier, safe
Facilities dining rooms, bar, swimming pool
Credit cards AE, DC, MC, V
Children welcome
Disabled access difficult
Pets accepted
Closed mid-Nov to mid-Dec
Proprietors Stefan and Susanne Urthaler

Trentino-Alto Adige

Turm

A solid former courthouse dating from the 12thC, with views across pastures and mountains, Hotel Turm offers typical Tyrolean hospitality with style and warmth. Bedrooms are all different and vary considerably in size, but even the smallest has everything you could want for a comfortable stay, including traditional furniture and somewhere cosy to sit. Our inspector's little room was enlivened by a charming group of naive paintings; another has a working ceramic stove, another a huge pine four-poster. The mini-apartments in particular are excellent value: one, in a little stone tower, is done as a wood-panelled *stübe*, with spiral staircase to a double room and a children's room. The Pramstrahler family's fine collection of contemporary art is displayed in every room and spills out along the whitewashed corridor walls.

The main dining room is light and spacious, with low wood ceiling and windows overlooking the valley; or you can dine in a romantic little room with heavy cast-iron door at the base of the 11thC tower. Either way, the elegantly presented food, cooked by Stefan Pramstrahler, who trained in France, is superb.

Nearby Val Gardena; Bolzano (16 km); Castelrotto (10 km).

Piazza della Chiesa 9, 39050 Fié allo Sciliar, Bolzano
Tel (0471) 725014
Fax (0471) 725474
Location in village, 16 km E of Bolzano, with garden and limited parking
Meals breakfast, lunch, dinner
Prices rooms L85,000–L305,000; standard double L185,000–L305,000; apartments L79,000–L230,000; breakfast included; dinner from L45,000
Rooms 28; 21 double and twin, 6 with bath, 15 with shower; 2 single with shower; 5 apartments with kitchen, 3 with shower, 2 with bath; all rooms have phone, TV, minibar, hairdrier, safe **Facilities** sitting room, dining rooms, bar, lift, garden, sauna, indoor and outdoor swimming pools **Credit cards** MC, V **Children** accepted **Disabled** access to public rooms **Pets** accepted **Closed** Nov to mid-Dec **Proprietor** Karl Pramstrahler

Trentino-Alto Adige

Der Pünthof

Via Claudio Augusto, a Roman road to Germany, passed what is now the entrance to Der Pünthof, and the watchtower built to guard the road forms an integral part of the hotel. The main building was a medieval farmhouse and has been in the Wolf family since the 17thC. They opened it as a hotel 40 years ago, housing guests in the barn, but over the decades other buildings have been added. Although Lagundo is a rather dreary suburb of Merano, once inside the hotel's electronic barrier you could be miles from anywhere with only orchards, vineyards and stunning scenery in view.

The public rooms are in the old building: breakfast is served in a pale green *stübe* with wooden floor, low ceiling, ceramic stove and traces of the original decoration on the panelled walls. Bedrooms in the barn are modern and comfortable, but uniform, though some have private terraces on to the garden. The most appealing are the rooms in the square tower. One has polished floorboards, a wood ceiling and antique bed. There are five well-equipped self-catering chalets, and six simpler cheaper rooms in another annexe.

Nearby Bolzano (28 km); Brennero (70 km); Dolomites.

Via Steinach 25, 39022 Lagundo, Bolzano **Tel** (0473) 448553 **Fax** (0473) 449919 **Location** 3 km NW of Merano, outside village; in own grounds with ample parking **Meals** breakfast, dinner **Prices** rooms L100,000–L190,000; standard double L120,000–L140,000; breakfast and dinner included (half board obligatory in high season)	**Rooms** 18; 16 double and twin, 2 with bath, 14 with shower; 2 single, 1 with bath, 1 with shower; most rooms have phone, TV, minibar, safe **Facilities** 2 breakfast rooms, sitting room, bar, restaurant, sauna, solarium, garden, tennis courts, swimming pool **Credit cards** AE, DC, MC, V **Children** accepted **Disabled** 1 room on ground floor **Pets** accepted **Closed** Nov to mid-Mar **Proprietors** Wolf family

Trentino-Alto Adige

Oberwirt

The building is typical of the area: solid, whitewashed, red-shuttered, with all sorts of arches and architectural ins and outs, and a crucifix and painted sundial on the front. Inside, public rooms are in traditional Tyrolean style with a profusion of wood panelling, carved furniture and nick-nacks; bedrooms, however, lack character: comfortable, spacious, mostly with balcony or terrace, but no traditional touches.

Originally a simple inn, Oberwirt has been run by the Waldner family since 1749. Today, three generations currently work in the hotel: Signor Waldner's beaming mother, dressed in a *dirndl*, is at reception, while his daughter runs the bar. The hotel is often full, and though it has plenty to recommend it, character and intimacy are not strong features – the misty 'romantic' photo on the cover of the brochure somehow says it all.

The highlight is the food. Our reporter gushed: 'Local produce ... creative presentation ... melt in the mouth pan-fried duck liver, lamb cutlets in a herb crust ... and the best pudding I've ever tasted (well almost): *marscapone* and compote of bitter cherries between wafer thin layers of strudel pastry.'

Nearby Passirio river and valley; Tirolo castle; Dolomites.

Vicolo San Felice 2, Marlengo, 39020 Merano, Bolzano
Tel (0473) 222020
Fax (0473) 447130
Location in village, 4 km SW of Merano; parking in garage or car park
Meals breakfast, lunch, dinner
Prices rooms L110,000–L344,000; standard double L220,000–L280,000; breakfast included; dinner from L50,000
Rooms 40; 34 double and twin, suites and junior suites, 6 single, all with bath or shower; all rooms have phone, TV, minibar, hairdrier, safe
Facilities sitting rooms, dining rooms, bar, meeting room, terrace, garden, indoor and outdoor swimming pools, sauna/solarium, tennis, riding, golf **Credit cards** AE, DC, MC, V
Children accepted
Disabled access to public rooms
Pets accepted **Closed** mid-Nov to mid-Mar **Proprietor** Joseph Waldner and family

Trentino-Alto Adige

Castel Fragsburg

A lovely drive along a narrow country lane, through mixed woodland and past Alpine pastures, brings you to the east of Merano where Castel Fragsburg – 300 years old and a hotel for more than 100 years – commands splendid views of the Texel massif. Externally, Fragsburg still looks very much the hunting lodge, with carved wooden shutters and balconies. A terrace along the entire front of the house, covered in wistaria, is a wonderful place to eat or drink: you seem to be suspended over the mountainside. The adjoining dining room offers Italian, Tyrolean and vegetarian menus and has huge picture windows which open up to become part of the terrace.

When we visited the hotel, it had just opened after a major refurbishment, and the updated interior sparkled: you can choose from various Tyrolean-style sitting rooms and a congenial little library. The bedrooms all have balconies, carved pine furniture and colourful country fabrics. The old cellars now contain a sauna and a gym. The wooded gardens, home to two tame mountain goats, provide plenty of space for lazing. A great choice for a holiday.

Nearby Passirio valley; Schloss Rametz.

Via Fragsburg 3, PO Box 210, 39012 Merano, Bolzano
Tel (0473) 244071
Fax (0473) 244493
Location 6 km NE of Merano; in own gardens with ample parking
Meals breakfast, lunch, dinner
Prices half board L130,000–L200,000 per person per day
Rooms 18; 13 double and twin, 11 with bath, 2 with shower; 2 single, one with bath, one with shower; 3 suites with bath; all rooms have phone, TV, hairdrier, safe
Facilities sitting rooms, dining rooms, library, sauna, gym, terrace, garden, swimming pool
Credit cards not accepted
Children accepted
Disabled 1 specially adapted room
Pets accepted
Closed Nov to Easter
Proprietors Ortner family

Trentino-Alto Adige

Converted castle, Merano

Castel Labers

On a hillside to the east of Merano, Castel (or Schloss) Labers is immersed in its own lush orchards and vineyards, with direct access to mountain walks through Alpine pastures. The hotel has been in the Neubert family since 1885, but the building itself dates back to the 11thC.

On a bad day, the Castel wouldn't look out of place in an Addams family film, but it has its charm, and the interior is welcoming with an impressive stone staircase with wrought-iron balustrades leading from the arched entrance hall up to the bedrooms. These vary enormously in size and standard: some elegantly proportioned with antique furniture, others rather too drab and basically furnished. The best rooms have balconies, particularly those on the corners; an attic room in the tower with a wood-panelled alcove is also charming.

The castle gardens are packed with trees and flowering shrubs, which can be admired from the conservatory restaurant; there are two other dining rooms, one baronial, with vaulted wooden ceiling. And the ambience? 'Elderly', writes a recent guest. 'Very pleasant, very quiet, but elderly.'

Nearby Passirio river and valley; Tirolo Castle; Dolomites.

Via Labers 25, 39012 Merano, Bolzano
Tel (0473) 234484
Fax (0473) 234146
Location 2.5 km E of Merano; with private grounds, garage and parking (locked at night)
Meals breakfast, lunch, dinner
Prices rooms L90,000–L280,000; standard double L180,000–L280,000; breakfast included; dinner from L50,000
Rooms 41; 22 double and twin, 20 with bath, 2 with shower; 9 single, 2 with bath, 7 with shower; 10 family with bath; all rooms have phone, safe; TV on request **Facilities** 3 dining rooms, music/reading room, bar, billiard room, conference room, lift, tennis court, swimming pool, garden
Credit cards AE, DC, MC, V
Children accepted
Disabled access difficult
Pets accepted **Closed** Nov to April **Proprietors** Stapf-Neubert family

Trentino-Alto Adige

Villa Tivoli

Almost in countryside, standing in apple orchards, the pale yellow villa is surrounded by an 'exquisite' terraced garden filled with over 2,000 different plants. Inside all is cool and chic, spacious and light, yet not intimidating. The ground floor is open-plan, with a glass-walled dining room; over the bar an extraordinary contemporary fresco of many-breasted Artemis, a recurring theme in the hotel. Another corner holds a sitting area, elegantly furnished with antiques and there is a traditional wood-panelled Tyrolean *stübe*. Outside, a terrace with tables shaded by yellow umbrellas, and in the basement, a pool room with gaily painted walls. Bedrooms are all different, all comfortable, with south-facing balconies. Some are huge, with separate sitting areas; some are furnished with antiques, others are very contemporary. Bathrooms are large, with double basins. Our reporter was hooked: 'Smart but relaxed; staff warm and welcoming, owners genuinely friendly and aiming to please; mountainous breakfast buffet, designed to see you through till evening, and a delicious dinner (half board includes five courses) accompanied by excellent local wines.'

Nearby Passirio river promenades; Passirio valley; Dolomites.

Via Verde 72, 39012 Merano, Bolzano
Tel (0473) 446282
Fax (0473) 446849
Location on edge of town; in own grounds with ample parking
Meals breakfast, lunch, dinner
Prices rooms L100,000–L316,000; standard double L160,000–L260,000; breakfast included; dinner from L50,000
Rooms 23; 14 double, 7 with bath, 7 with shower; 5 single with shower; 4 suites with bath; all rooms have phone, TV, hairdrier
Facilities sitting room, dining room, bar, indoor swimming pool, lift, terrace, garden
Credit cards AE, DC, MC, V
Children accepted
Disabled access difficult
Pets accepted
Closed mid-Nov to mid-Mar
Proprietors Defranceschi family

Trentino-Alto Adige

Schloss Korb

Rising up above the fertile vineyards and orchards that surround the outskirts of Bolzano is the 11thC tower which forms the centrepiece of Schloss Korb.

The entrance to the hotel is a riot of colour – flowering shrubs and plants set against walls of golden stone and whitewash. Inside, furnishings and decorations are in traditional style, and antiques and fresh flowers abound. Reception is a cool, dark, tiled hall set about with a most eccentric collection of objects including carvings, golden angels on the walls, huge plants, busts, heavy mirrors, brass ornaments and armoury – the oldest part of the hotel. Surrounding the main restaurant is a terrace, hanging out over the valley and awash with plants, where breakfast and drinks can be enjoyed. The feel of the place is relaxed, though not intimate.

The bedrooms in the castle are generous in size, with separate sitting areas and lovely views out over the vineyards. Best are those in the tower, or the traditional apartment with its carved furniture. Rooms in the annexe all have balconies, and here there is a lift and an indoor heated pool.

Nearby Bolzano (8 km); Merano (36 km); Dolomites.

Missiano, 39050 San Paolo, Bolzano
Tel (0471) 636000
Fax (0471) 636033
Location 8 km W of Bolzano, in gardens; ample parking
Meals breakfast, lunch, dinner
Prices rooms L100,000–L380,000; standard double L200,000–L300,000; breakfast included; dinner from L55,000
Rooms 62; 54 double and twin, 2 single, all with bath; 6 suites, 5 with bath, one with shower; all rooms have phone, TV; half the rooms have safe
Facilities sitting rooms, dining room, bar, sauna, beauty salon, conference rooms, terraces, garden, tennis courts, indoor and outdoor swimming pools
Credit cards not accepted
Children accepted
Disabled access difficult
Pets accepted
Closed Nov to Mar
Proprietors Dellago family

Trentino-Alto Adige

Mountain chalet, Ortisei

Uhrerhof Deur

The name means 'House of the Clocks', and their ticking and chiming, along with birdsong, are very often the only sounds which break the silence at this traditional chalet set in a tucked-away hamlet 1,600 metres above sea level. Outside, there is a grassy garden from which to enjoy the wide and wonderful view and perhaps watch the mountain goats who come and nibble flowers in the window boxes. Inside, all the rooms, including the balconied bedrooms, are bright, simple and beautifully kept, with plenty of homely details. The core of the chalet is 400 years old, and includes the all-wood *stübe* with working stove. The three adjoining dining rooms have wooden benches round the walls, Tyrolean fabrics for curtains and cushions, bright rugs on terracotta floors and pewter plates displayed in wall racks. Signor Zemmer is the chef, much of the produce coming from his own vegetable garden. Even the potato crisps are home-made.

Underneath the house is a surprisingly smart health complex, with huge picture windows so that you can relax in the open-plan Turkish bath and soak up the view. Strictly no smoking in the *pensione*.

Nearby Val Gardena; Castelrotto (13 km); Bolzano (26 km).

Bulla, 39046 Ortisei, Bolzano
Tel (0471) 797335
Fax (0471) 797457
Location in mountainside hamlet, 13 km E of Castelrotto, off Castelrotto–Ortisei road; garage parking
Meals breakfast, dinner
Prices half board (obligatory for rooms, not for apartments) double room L220,000–L300,000; single room L120,000–L160,000; breakfast included; dinner from L50,000

Rooms 11; 5 double and twin, 4 with bath, 1 with shower; 2 single with shower; 4 apartments for 2 to 5 people with kitchen, living room; all rooms have phone, TV, hairdrier, safe **Facilities** dining room, bar, sitting room, garden, health centre **Credit cards** MC, V **Children** accepted **Disabled** not suitable **Pets** not accepted **Closed** Nov, 2 weeks after Easter **Proprietors** Zemmer family

Trentino-Alto Adige

Castel Pergine

This medieval hilltop fortress has been managed with love and enthusiasm for the past five years by an energetic and cultured Swiss couple. Past and present coexist happily in a rather alternative atmosphere, and the castle has a truly lived-in feel despite its grand dimensions and impressive history.

The route from the car park to the hotel leads you under stone arches, up age-worn steps and through vaulted chambers to the airy, round reception hall where breakfast is also served. The two spacious dining rooms afford wonderful views, and the light, innovative cooking, based on the regional cuisine, has earned two crossed forks from Michelin. The bedrooms are by no means luxurious, and some are very small, but all are furnished in simple good taste; the best have splendid, heavy, carved wooden furniture and wall panelling.

One of the most enchanting features of the castle is the walled garden. Spend an hour reading a book, or simply watching the mountains through the crumbling ramparts, and you may never want to leave.

Nearby Trento (11 km); Lake Caldonazzo (3 km); Segonzano (20 km).

38057 Pergine, Valsugana, Trento
Tel (0461) 531158
Fax (0461) 531329
Location off the SS47 Padua road, 2 km SE of Pergine; in own grounds with ample parking
Meals breakfast, dinner
Prices rooms L75,000–L160,000; standard double L160,000; breakfast included; dinner from L40,000
Rooms 21; 13 double and twin, 8 with shower; 4 single, 3 with shower; 4 triple, 3 with shower; all rooms have phone
Facilities sitting room, dining rooms, bar, garden
Credit cards AE, MC, V
Children welcome
Disabled access difficult
Pets accepted
Closed Nov to Thursday before Easter
Proprietors Verena and Theo Schneider-Neff

Trentino-Alto Adige

Ansitz Heufler

The word 'ansitz' means unfortified aristocratic residence and this one, dating from the 16thC, is a beautiful example. Although set rather incongruously on the edge of an unremarkable village, it is surrounded by stunning scenery. The hotel has featured in our all-Italy guide for many years, but has recently changed hands. Our inspector felt that though alterations made by the new owners are subtle, they are not all beneficial. The rooms look fresh, but some have been changed around so that the main sitting room, a superbly carved old *stübe*, is now practically devoid of furniture and only used for receptions. The profusion of beribboned candles, lace cushions and teddy bears in alcoves were too pretty-pretty for her taste.

The food served in the three wood-panelled dining rooms is no longer solid Tyrolean fare, but leans strongly towards the *nouvelle*. The bar is in the original smokery with blackened walls and vaulted ceiling. The bedrooms are all different, full of marvellous furniture and architectural features, but beware of hitting your head on low lintels. A lovely hotel, whose soul has unfortunately been compromised by the recent prettifying.
Nearby Brunico (10 km).

Rasun di Sopra 37, 39030 Rasun, Anterselva
Tel (0474) 498582
Fax (0474) 498046
Location in village in wooded Anterselva valley, 10 km E of Brunico; in own grounds with parking
Meals breakfast, lunch, dinner
Prices rooms L98,000–L296,000; standard double L196,000; breakfast included; dinner from L60,000
Rooms 8; 5 double and twin, 2 with bath, 3 with shower; 3 suites, 2 with bath, 1 with shower; all rooms have phone
Facilities sitting rooms, sitting areas, dining rooms, bar, garden,
Credit cards AE, DC, MC, V
Children accepted
Disabled not suitable
Pets not accepted
Closed mid-Nov to Dec, mid-Apr to May
Proprietor Johann Oberhammer

Trentino-Alto Adige

Mountain hotel, Redagno di Sopra

Zirmerhof

Situated just outside the tiny hamlet of Redagno di Sopra, this 12thC *mas* has been in the Perwanger family since 1890. Views are of mountains, green pastures and forests with few signs of civilization to mar the landscape. The interior has been carefully and tastefully restored. The dim, low-ceilinged hall with its intricate wood carving, ticking grandfather clock and old fireplace, immediately plunges you into the atmosphere of an old family home. There is a tiny cosy library, a sitting-cum-breakfast room with an open fire for winter days, and a rustic bar with a grassy terrace, from which to enjoy the superb views. The large wood-panelled dining room houses two elaborate ceramic stoves, and makes a fine setting in which to enjoy the local dishes and sophisticated wines on offer.

The comfortable bedrooms vary enormously in size, but all are attractive with traditional carved furniture (much of it made on the premises) and pretty fabrics; the largest rooms are on the top floor. For the energetic, there's plenty to do, particularly in winter, from skating and curling on the lake to cross-country and downhill skiing.

Nearby Cavalese (15 km).

39040 Redagno, Bolzano
Tel (0471) 887215
Fax (0471) 887225
Location 5 km N of Fontanefredde, off the SS48; in garden with ample parking
Meals breakfast, lunch, dinner
Prices rooms L70,000–L304,000; standard double L120,000–L268,000; breakfast included; dinner from L40,000
Rooms 31; 23 double and twin, 2 with bath, 21 with shower; 7 single, 2 with bath, 5 with shower; 1 suite with shower; rooms have TV on request
Facilities dining room, sitting room, bar, library, garden
Credit cards AE, DC, MC, V
Children accepted
Disabled ground-floor bedrooms available
Pets accepted
Closed early Nov to day after Christmas, after Easter to mid-May
Proprietor Sepp Perwanger

Trentino-Alto Adige

Country guest-house, San Osvaldo

Gasthof Tschötscherhof

Don't be put off by the unpronounceable name; for lovers of simple, farmhouse accommodation in an unspoilt rural setting, this hostelry could be ideal. The narrow road from Siusi winds through apple orchards, vineyards and open meadows, eventually arriving at the tiny hamlet of San Osvaldo and this typical 500-year-old farmhouse with its adjacent dark wood barn. The name, painted on the outside of the building, is almost hidden by the clambering vines, and the old wooden balconies are a colourful riot of cascading geraniums. The sun-drenched terrace is a perfect spot for relaxing and eating.

Inside, we were assailed by inviting smells from the kitchen at the end of the hall, and were drawn to the warmth of the low-ceilinged old *stübe* with its gently ticking clock, rough wood floor and simple white ceramic stove.

A rustic stone stairway leads up to the modest but tidy bedrooms, some of which have balconies. They have no frills, but after a long day in glorious countryside, we were too tired to notice on our return.

Nearby Castelrotto (5 km); Bolzano (17 km); Sciliar Natural Park (10 km).

San Osvaldo 19, 39040 Siuisi, Bolzano
Tel/Fax (0471) 706013
Location in hamlet, 5 km W of Castelrotto; with parking
Meals breakfast, lunch, dinner
Prices rooms L38,000–L76,000; standard double L76,000; breakfast included; dinner L25,000–L30,000
Rooms 8; 7 double and twin, 1 single, all with shower
Facilities dining rooms, terrace
Credit cards not accepted

Children welcome
Disabled access difficult
Pets accepted
Closed Dec to Mar
Proprietors Jaider family

Trentino-Alto Adige

Mountain guest-house, San Valburga d'Ultimo

Eggwirt

The quiet and unspoilt Val d'Ultima lies 30 kilometres south-west of Merano. An ideal setting for both summer and winter sports, the Gasthof Eggwirt has existed as a hostelry since the 14thC, and today the Schwienbacher family welcome guests as if to their own home. The hotel is on the edge of the village with a large terrace at the front and superb views all around. The long life of the house is best felt in the *stübe* which dates from 1611: entirely panelled in dark wood with an old ceramic stove in the corner and stags' heads on the walls, this room was a favourite haunt of Sir Herbert Dunhill (a regular guest), and his black and white photographs are on display. A larger room housing a little bar has a country feel to it, with a ticking clock and rough, bare floorboards (which are scrubbed daily).

Upstairs, the decoration is more modern, less personal. The bright bedrooms have lots of wood and cheerful duvet covers. Some of the larger ones are divided, and most have balconies with, of course, stunning views. We should mention that this inexpensive, relaxed and friendly family hotel offers some excellent ski deals for the children.

Nearby Merano (30 km).

39016 San Valburga d'Ultimo, Bolzano
Tel (0473) 795319
Fax (0473) 795471
Location 35 km SW of Merano, off SS238, in village; parking
Meals breakfast, lunch, dinner
Prices rooms L50,000–L96,000; standard double L96,000; breakfast included; dinner from L30,000
Rooms 20; 11 double and twin, 10 with shower, 1 with bath; 3 single with shower; 4 triple, 2 with bath, 2 with shower, 2 family with shower; all rooms have phone, TV on request, safe
Facilities restaurant, sitting room, bar, terraces
Credit cards not accepted
Children welcome
Disabled not suitable
Pets accepted
Closed 10 Nov to 24 Dec
Proprietor Schwienbacher family

Trentino-Alto Adige

Bad Ratzes

Leaving the small town of Siusi in search of Bad Ratzes, the road winds uphill past green meadows and into a dense forest where Hansel and Gretel would have felt at home. When at last you reach it in a clearing, the hotel, large and modern, looks disconcertingly grim, but the warmth and enthusiasm of the Scherlin sisters will put you immediately at ease. Inside, the decoration is dull 1960s and 1970s, but comfortable. Public areas – including a formal sitting room with open fireplace, a children's playroom, and two dining rooms – are extensive. All but four of the spotless bedrooms have balconies.

Food is important at Bad Ratzes: local dishes are carefully prepared and pasta is home-made. One of the sisters bakes regularly, and her recipes are recorded in a little booklet. This is one of a group of family hotels in the area and there are many thoughtful child-orientated extras: pots of crayons and paper on the dining tables, a booklet of local bedtime stories, walks for children, a special menu and so on. Adults are not neglected; there is wonderful and varied walking in the neighbourhood and a free ski bus runs to the slopes in winter.

Nearby Bolzano (22 km); Siusi National Park; skiing (10 km).

Razzes, 39040 Siusi allo Sciliar, Bolzano
Tel (0471) 706131
Fax (0471) 706131
Location 22 km NE of Bolzano, 3 km SE of Siusi; in own grounds with ample parking
Meals breakfast, lunch, dinner
Prices half board L89,000–L132,000 per person
Rooms 52; 36 double, 9 single, 7 family rooms, all with bath; all rooms have phone, hairdrier; 18 rooms have TV and safe

Facilities dining rooms, sitting rooms, bar, playroom, indoor swimming pool, sauna, garden, garage
Credit cards not accepted
Children welcome
Disabled not suitable
Pets accepted
Closed Sunday after Easter to mid-May
Proprietors Scherlin family

Trentino-Alto Adige

Town hotel, Trento

Accademia

Favoured by showbiz types, this upmarket hotel is run by two lively sisters and their efficient staff, and occupies an attractive medieval house on a tiny street in the old centre of Trento. Quaint wooden shutters and geranium-filled window boxes break up the four storeys of elegant cream stucco façade. Inside, elements of the original architecture are also visible: a stone stairway leading up from reception, doorways and vaulted ceilings. The building's clean white lines are enlivened by vibrant rugs, parquet floors and strategically placed antiques.

The atmosphere is carried through to the bright, airy bedrooms, decorated predominantly in blue and white. Some have a rustic air, varnished wood floors and attic ceilings. The wood-panelled suite at the top is particularly appealing, furnished with smart modern sofas, colourful kilims and modern prints.

The restaurant – a white vaulted room, with crisp tablecloths – serves interesting, creative food. There is also a homely *enoteca*, where you can taste a wide range of local wines or have a snack. Breakfast is a particular pleasure when taken on the walled terrace, shaded by a giant horse-chestnut tree.

Nearby Santa Maria; Piazza del Duomo.

Vicolo Colico 4–6, 38100 Trento
Tel (0461) 233600
Fax (0461) 230174
Location in old part of town between Duomo and Piazza Dante; with free parking nearby
Meals breakfast, lunch, dinner
Prices rooms L150,000–L445,000; standard double L210,000–L250,000; breakfast included; dinner from L40,000
Rooms 43; 32 double and twin, 16 with bath, 16 with shower; 9 single with shower; 2 suites with bath; all rooms have phone, TV, air-conditioning, minibar, hairdrier
Facilities sitting rooms, restaurant, *enoteca*, terrace
Credit cards AE, DC, MC, V
Children accepted
Disabled no special facilities
Pets accepted
Closed Christmas to early Jan, restaurant Monday
Proprietors Fambri family

San Marco

Town hotel

Alcyone

Recently renovated, this was formerly an old-fashioned *pensione* called the Brooklyn. Though the new owners are proud of their make-over, one suspects that the old hotel had more character because the parts which have been left intact are charming. The pretty little breakfast room has waist-high painted panelling with gold velvet above, dotted with ceramic plates; the stairwell is similar. The newly decorated sugar-almond pink bedrooms are very small, done out in standard Venice hotel style: purpose made painted furniture, Murano glass wall lights, silk damask bedcovers. Prices are ambitious.

Nearby Piazza San Marco; San Zulian.

Calle dei Fabbri, San Marco 4712, 30124 Venezia
Tel (041) 5212508
Fax (041) 5212942
Location in shopping street, 2 mins walk from Piazza San Marco; **vaporetto** San Marco, Rialto or water taxi
Meals breakfast
Prices rooms L90,000–L280,000; standard double
L280,000; breakfast included
Rooms 21; 19 double and twin, 2 single, 2 with bath, 19 with shower; all rooms have phone, TV, air-conditioning, hairdrier
Facilities breakfast room
Children accepted
Disabled not suitable
Pets accepted
Closed never
Proprietor Alessio Ricchi

Town hotel

Bel Sito & Berlino

The Bel Sito has its charms, including a flowery patio right on the *campo*, and given a sympathetic facelift one feels it could make a fine hotel. Too many of the rooms, however (they vary greatly), are small, skimpily furnished and worn at the edges, and the extensive reception rooms look dowdy (although the long, mirrored breakfast room retains its old-fashioned dignity). Nos 30 and 40 have little balconies and wonderful close-up views of the exuberant baroque façade of Santa Maria Zobenigo, but they need updating and redecoration. Best are the rooms with views on to the canal.

Nearby Piazza San Marco; Teatro La Fenice.

Campo Santa Maria del Giglio, San Marco 2517, 30124 Venezia
Tel (041) 5223365 **Fax** (041) 5204083 **Location** between Piazza San Marco and Campo Santo Stefano; **vaporetto** Santa Maria del Giglio or water taxi
Meals breakfast **Prices** rooms L115,000–L347,000; standard double L190,000–L275,000; breakfast included **Rooms** 38
double, twin, triple and single, all with bath or shower; all rooms have phone, TV, hairdrier; air-conditioning units on request **Facilities** sitting room, breakfast room, bar, terrace **Credit cards** AE, MC, V **Children** accepted **Disabled** access difficult **Pets** accepted **Closed** never **Proprietor** Luigi Gino Serafini

San Marco

Town hotel

Centauro

A hotel that has been in existence since the 17thC, and in the Tomasutti family for much of the 20thC. Riccardo has broken away from tradition however, and transformed what was a slightly dingy two star. Flock wallpaper has been jettisoned in favour of glossy paint effects; beams have been washed dark red with a yellow motif; the huge doors painted pale green. Only the cavernous breakfast room, with half-panelled walls and parquet floor, so far remains intact. Bedrooms, six with canal views, are airy with white walls, high ceilings, Venetian marble floors and fabric-covered furniture.
Nearby Bovolo staircase; Teatro La Fenice; Rialto Bridge.

Calle D. Vida, Campo Manin, San Marco 4297/a, 30124 Venezia
Tel (041) 5225832 **Fax** (041) 5239151 **Location** in little street to the S of the square; **vaporetto** Rialto **Meals** breakfast **Prices** rooms L75,000–L215,000; standard double L108,000–L215,000; breakfast included **Rooms** 31; 18 double and twin, all with bath or shower; 6 single with shower; 6 triple and family, 1 suite, all with bath or shower; all rooms have phone; some have TV, minibar **Facilities** breakfast room, sitting area **Credit cards** AE, DC, MC, V **Children** accepted **Disabled** not suitable **Pets** accepted **Closed** Nov to Jan **Proprietor** Ricardo Tomasutti

---

Town hotel

Do Pozzi

In a tiny palm-fringed courtyard, where café tables and chairs spill on to the pavement in summer, this hotel has the twin advantages of a quiet central location and its own restaurant, 'da Raffaele', specializing in Venetian cuisine and prettily set on a side canal. But our inspector's high expectations were disappointed by the dull interior; acres of silk damask cover the walls and furnishings are standard throughout. She regretted that there were not more original touches like the icons in the outer breakfast room. Some bedrooms look tatty, others are serviceable; bathrooms are 'excruciatingly small'.
Nearby Santa Maria del Giglio; Teatro La Fenice.

Calle Larga 22 Marzo, San Marco 2373, 30124 Venezia
Tel (041) 5207855 **Fax** (041) 5229413 **Location** in courtyard S of Calle Larga 22 Marzo; **vaporetto** Santa Maria del Giglio, San Marco **Meals** breakfast **Prices** rooms L120,000–L250,000; standard double L180,000–L250,000; breakfast included **Rooms** 30; 25 double and twin, all with bath or shower; 5 single with shower; all rooms have phone, TV, air-conditioning, minibar, hairdrier **Facilities** 2 breakfast/sitting rooms, restaurant, lift **Credit cards** AE, DC, MC, V **Children** accepted **Disabled** no special facilities **Pets** accepted **Closed** never **Proprietor** Stefania Salmaso

San Marco

Town hotel

Kette

Refurbished a few years ago in an ambitiously formal style of faux marble and much wood panelling, the Kette now has a disappointingly institutional feel. Displays of Murano glass and a few *objets d'art* add some personality. Bedrooms are traditional, with a masculine touch – dark wood furniture, carved headboards, plain fabrics. The second-floor breakfast room is elegant, with circular tables and unusual tube-shaped armchairs; there is also a soulless TV room packed with tables and chairs which can't often be used. The hotel is ideally positioned, backing on to a canal near Campo San Fantin.

Nearby Teatro La Fenice; Piazza San Marco.

Piscina San Moisè, San Marco 2053, 30124 Venezia **Tel** (041) 5207766 **Fax** (041) 5228964 **Location** 5 mins walk from Piazza San Marco, near Campo San Fantin; **vaporetto** San Marco or water taxi **Meals** breakfast **Prices** rooms L150,000–L320,000; standard double L250,000–L320,000; breakfast included **Rooms** 65; 58 double, twin and triple, 7 singles; 29 with bath, 29 with shower; all rooms have phone, TV, air-conditioning, minibar, hairdrier, safe **Facilities** breakfast room, TV room, lift **Credit cards** AE, DC, MC, V **Children** accepted **Disabled** access difficult **Pets** accepted **Closed** never **Proprietor** Signor Baessato

---

Town hotel

Monaco & Grand Canal

A traditional grand hotel with all the trappings including plush Venetian-style furnishings, impeccably uniformed footmen, and multilingual receptionists, who are perfectly charming so long as you're a VIP. Its attractions are the location, right on the Grand Canal, with magical views across to Salute and San Giorgio Maggiore, and masses of space downstairs to sit in comfortable armchairs and enjoy them. The drawback, we've heard, is noise from *vaporetti* chugging past, which disturbs the first-floor rooms at the front. Go for a room – or suite, if you can afford it – on an upper floor.

Nearby Piazza San Marco.

Calle Vallaresso, San Marco 1325, 30124 Venezia **Tel** (041) 5200211 **Fax** (041) 5200501 **Location** right on Grand Canal to W of Piazza San Marco; **vaporetto** San Marco **Meals** breakfast, lunch, dinner **Prices** rooms L220,000–L650,000; standard double L340,000–L650,000; breakfast included **Rooms** 70; 64 double and twin and single, 6 suites, all with bath; all rooms have phone, TV, air-conditioning, minibar, hairdrier, safe **Facilities** breakfast room, sitting rooms, restaurant, bar, lift, terrace **Credit cards** AE, DC, MC, V **Children** accepted **Disabled** no special facilities **Pets** accepted **Closed** never **Manager** Giuseppe Vacciano

San Marco

Apartments in private house

Palazzetto Pisani

The vast Palazzo Pisani is now the Conservatory of Music, while the doge's descendants still inhabit this adjacent *palazzetto* on the Grand Canal. Times have changed, and now you can rent the fabulous *piano nobile* while the present incumbents retire to private rooms. There are two bedrooms, one grand, one simple, a beautiful drawing room overlooking the canal, and two dining rooms where you can hold parties. The one-bedroom ground-floor apartment has a wonderful original bathroom. The grandeur may be faded, but this is a rare opportunity to masquerade for a while as a Venetian aristocrat.
Nearby Accademia gallery; Piazza San Marco.

Calle di Ca' Genova, San Marco 2814, 30124 Venezia **Tel** (041) 5285343 **Fax** (041) 5232550 **Location** corner of Grand Canal and Rio dell'Orso, off Campo Santo Stefano; **vaporetto** Accademia or water taxi **Meals** can be provided by arrangement **Prices** on application **Rooms** ground-floor suite with 1 double bedroom, ante-room, kitchen, bathroom; *piano nobile* with 2 double bedrooms, bathroom, shower room, 2 sitting rooms, 2 dining rooms, gallery, kitchen **Facilities** maid service, cook available **Credit cards** not accepted **Children** well-behaved children accepted **Pets** on ground floor only **Closed** never **Proprietor** Contessa Maria Pia Ferre

---

Apartments

Palazzo del Giglio

This handsome converted mansion contains 19 smart flats to rent on a daily or weekly basis. Size varies from one-room studios to a penthouse that sleeps five with a roof terrace (No. 401). Price depends not just on the size of the apartment and length of your stay, but also on the time of year, number of people, and whether it has a view. All elegantly decorated in a similar style, the comfortable rooms are well furnished with a mix of the traditional and the ultra-modern. Cleverly designed kitchens are tucked into tiny spaces. Bathrooms are of sparkling Carrara marble, some with jacuzzis.
Nearby Santa Maria del Giglio; Teatro La Fenice.

Campo Santa Maria del Giglio, San Marco, 30124 Venezia **Tel** (041) 2719111 **Fax** (041) 5205158 **Location** just N of the Gritti Palace; **vaporetto** Santa Maria del Giglio **Meals** room-service breakfast **Prices** apartments L400,000–L1,100,000 **Rooms** 19 apartments: studio, one-bedroom and two-bedroom; all apartments have phone, TV, fax/modem point, air-conditioning, kitchen, hairdrier, safe **Facilities** maid service **Credit cards** AE, DC, MC, V **Children** accepted **Disabled** no special facilities **Pets** accepted **Closed** never **Manager** Maria Elena Fabiano

San Marco

Town hotel

Panada

The real attraction of this hotel is its bar. A couple of guests we met here agreed, saying it was the perfect place for a nightcap. Cosy and wood-panelled, with red velvet seats, it lives up to its name 'Ai Speci' ('of mirrors' in local dialect), as almost every inch of wall space is covered by antique looking-glasses. The hotel itself tends towards predictability. Pluses are a decent-sized and comfortable sitting area, and freshly decorated bedrooms with attractive painted furniture. Minuses are a staff who could muster only a cool welcome and an easy win in any 'most hideous breakfast room' contest.
Nearby Piazza San Marco; San Zulian.

Calle Specchieri, San Marco 646, 30124 Venezia
Tel (041) 5209088
Fax (041) 5209619
Location between Calle Larga San Marco and San Zulian; **vaporetto** San Marco
Meals breakfast
Prices rooms L180,000–L520,000; standard double L220,000–L380,000; breakfast included **Rooms** 48; 28 double and twin, 7 triple and family, 13 single, all with bath or shower; all rooms have phone, TV, air-conditioning, hairdrier, safe **Facilities** breakfast room, bar, sitting room, lift **Credit cards** AE, DC, MC, V **Children** accepted **Disabled** no special facilities **Pets** accepted **Closed** never **Manager** Maurizio Scarpa

Town hotel

Torino

A fine Gothic façade, flaunting splendid ogee windows, some impressive stuccoed ceilings, and a fusty feel are the last traces of the original 15thC *palazzo*. On the whole, the Torino is low-key by *palazzo* standards, with predictable decoration and modern furnishings. In keeping with its history, however, are the medieval-style reception desk, and the saintly statue which watches over guests as they eat a frugal breakfast. Bedrooms vary from huge, high-ceilinged first-floor rooms with swirling carpets and tall windows, to smaller, cosier pink rooms on the upper floors with rooftop views.
Nearby Santa Maria del Giglio; Teatro La Fenice.

Calle delle Ostreghe, San Marco 2356, 30124 Venezia
Tel (041) 5205222
Fax (041) 5228227
Location just W of Campo Santa Maria del Giglio; **vaporetto** Santa Maria del Giglio, San Marco
Meals breakfast **Prices** rooms L100,000–L320,000; standard double L180,000–L320,000; breakfast included **Rooms** 20; 19 double and twin, 1 single, all with shower; all rooms have phone, TV, air-conditioning, minibar, hairdrier, safe **Facilities** breakfast room, sitting area **Credit cards** AE, DC, MC, V **Children** accepted **Disabled** not possible **Pets** accepted **Closed** never **Manager** Claudio Vecchiato

San Marco

Town hotel

San Giorgio

If you want a quiet location, yet close to the bustling main thoroughfare between San Marco and Rialto, consider the San Giorgio, tucked down a side street next to the Museo Fortuny. Bedrooms are small, neat, well cared for, with bathrooms of varying sizes, some with large shower cubicles. One room has an attractive carved wardrobe, others have pretty examples of Venetian painted furniture. Downstairs is a large, rather dark sitting/breakfast room. While unremarkable, this is another example of a simple two-star hotel which gives better value for money than many a more expensive three star.

Nearby Piazza San Marco; Accademia gallery.

Rio Terrà della Mandola, San Marco 3781, 30124 Venezia **Tel** (041) 5235835 **Fax** (041) 5228072 **Location** off Calle della Mandola, close to Campo Sant' Angelo, between San Marco & Rialto; **vaporetto** Sant'Angelo **Meals** breakfast **Prices** rooms L120,000–L210,000; standard double L180,000–L210,000; breakfast included **Rooms** 16; 12 double/twin, 4 single, all with shower; all rooms have phone, TV, air-conditioning, hairdrier, safe **Facilities** sitting/breakfast room **Credit cards** AE, MC, V **Children** accepted **Disabled** not suitable **Pets** accepted **Closed** never **Proprietor** Renzo Cristofoli Prat

---

Town guest-house

San Zulian

A sensible little hotel where public rooms and corridors are painted white, with colourful pictures and furniture upholstered in smart red and white stripes. Bedrooms, though simple, are similarly fresh, well-equipped, with pretty green furniture and white tiled bathrooms with properly enclosed showers. Rooms vary in size, so try for a larger one. Only one breaks the mould, with a silk hanging above the bed and a charming ottoman at its foot. The 'honeymoon room' has a private terrace with views across the rooftops to the domes of San Marco (which compensates for the minute bathroom).

Nearby San Zulian; Santa Maria Formosa; Piazza San Marco.

Piscina San Zulian, San Marco 535, 30124 Venezia **Tel** (041) 5225872 **Fax** (041) 5232265 **Location** beside San Zulian church, between Piazza San Marco and Rialto; **vaporetto** San Marco **Meals** breakfast **Prices** rooms L100,000–L210,000; standard double L210,000; breakfast included **Rooms** 19, all double and twin or triple, all with shower; all rooms have phone, TV, air-conditioning, minibar, hairdrier, safe **Facilities** breakfast/sitting room **Credit cards** AE, DC, MC, V **Children** accepted **Disabled** not suitable **Pets** accepted **Closed** never **Proprietor** Mauro Girotto

Santa Croce

Town hotel

Falier

In a lively university neighbourhood, where students throng the streets, this well-placed straightforward two star is under the same ownership as the American (see page 52). Though lacking the character and flair of its better known sister, the Falier is decorated to a high standard. Pleasant public rooms are done out in subtle shades, with marble chequered floors, and there's a pretty terracotta-tiled courtyard for *al fresco* breakfasts. Identical-looking bedrooms have innocuous modern fittings, but there's one at the top with beams and a private roof terrace. At the same price as a standard double, it's a bargain.
Nearby Scuola Grande di San Rocco; Frari.

Salizzada San Pantalon, Santa Croce 130, 30135 Venezia
Tel (041) 710882/711005
Fax (041) 5206554
Location just W of the San Pantalon canal; **vaporetto** Piazzale Roma, San Tomà
Meals breakfast
Prices rooms L100,000–L210,000; standard double L130,000–L210,000; breakfast included **Rooms** 19; 14 double and twin, 5 single, all with shower; all rooms have phone, hairdrier **Facilities** breakfast room, sitting area, garden
Credit cards AE, MC, V
Children accepted **Disabled** no special facilities **Pets** accepted
Closed never
Proprietor Salvatore Sutera Sardo

Town hotel

Al Sole

This hotel occupies the 16thC *palazzo* Ca' Marcello, a lovely mellow brick buiding with narrow Gothic arches for windows, built on the dog-leg in the Rio dei Tolentini. The best bedrooms afford views down both stretches of the canal. Relics from its *palazzo* days include beamed ceilings supported by stone columns, and chequerboard marble floors. Unfortunately most of the furnishings date from 1971, when it was converted to a hotel – or look as if they do – and the bedrooms are drab. But there's a jolly bar on the ground floor with doors leading to a very pretty vine-shaded garden.
Nearby Scuola Grande di San Rocco; Frari.

Fondamenta Minotto, Santa Croce 136, 30135 Venezia
Tel (041) 710844
Fax (041) 714398
Location opposite Tolentini bridge; **vaporetto** Piazzale Roma or water taxi **Meals** breakfast, dinner **Prices** rooms L120,000–L320,000; standard double L190,000–L320,000; breakfast included; dinner from L28,000 **Rooms** 80; 63 double and twin, 17 single, all with bath or shower; all rooms have phone, TV, air-conditioning, minibar, hairdrier **Facilities** sitting areas, bar, restaurant, lift, garden **Credit cards** AE, DC, MC, V **Children** accepted **Disabled** no special facilities **Pets** accepted **Closed** never **Manager** Mario Scarpa

Castello

Town guest-house

Bucintoro

A simple, family-run *pensione* with few modern facilities, plain bedrooms and a glorious view across the San Marco Basin from almost every room. These are fairly dull but clean and acceptable. No. 4 is one of the pleasantest, with a large bed, pretty bedspread, airy curtains and the waters of the lagoon gently lapping below. The breakfast room and sitting room, with its grim velvet-covered furniture dominating the room, are both full of windows clad in frilly net curtains. The modest cement-rendered building with tables outside in summer is conveniently close to the *vaporetto* stop at Arsenale.
Nearby Arsenale; San Giovanni in Bragora.

Riva San Biagio, Castello 2135, 30122 Venezia **Tel** (041) 5223240 **Fax** (041) 5235224 **Location** on the waterfront, just past the Arsenale *vaporetto* stop **vaporetto** Arsenale, Tana **Meals** breakfast, dinner (Apr–Oct) **Prices** rooms L90,000–L210,000; standard double L185,000–L210,000; breakfast included; dinner L35,000 **Rooms** 28; 22 double, twin and triple, 17 with bath, 5 with shower; 6 single, 5 with shower, one with basin; all rooms have phone, fans on request, hairdrier **Facilities** breakfast room, sitting room, terrace **Credit cards** not accepted **Children** accepted **Disabled** not suitable **Pets** not accepted **Closed** Dec, Jan **Proprietor** Augusta Bianchi

---

Town hotel

Canada

Two rooms only are worth having here: the ones at the very top, each with its own wooden railed terrace looking out across tiled roofs and church façades to the *campanile* of St Mark's. Though simple and straightforward, their carved mahogany and studded velvet bedheads add a touch of pomp, and the bathrooms are clean and neat. They cost no more than any other room, but the bonus of the terrace makes them distinctly good value. You will have to climb endless stairs to reach reception, and yet more to get to the bedrooms so only the fit need apply. A simple hotel without much character, although we found the staff friendly.
Nearby Rialto; Santa Maria Formosa.

Campo San Lio, Castello 5659, 30122 Venezia **Tel** (041) 5229912 **Fax** (041) 5235852 **Location** in small square, midway between Rialto and Campo Santa Maria Formosa **vaporetto** Rialto **Meals** breakfast **Prices** rooms L80,000–L200,000; standard double L120,000–L200,000; breakfast included **Rooms** 25, all double and twin, 4 with bath, 21 with shower; all rooms have phone **Facilities** breakfast room **Credit cards** MC, V **Children** accepted **Disabled** not suitable **Pets** accepted **Closed** never **Proprietor** Signor Brusaferro

Castello

Town hotel

Paganelli

This modest, friendly place gives itself no airs at all – in fact the wood-veneer-clad entrance, filled with leather chairs, looks remarkably unprepossessing – but it shares the same lagoon views as much more august and expensive hotels on the Riva. And the simple pleasant bedrooms far exceed the public rooms. They are furnished with pretty, delicate, painted pieces, and gauze curtains flutter at the shuttered windows. Largest and smartest rooms face the waterfront: No. 6 is our favourite. Breakfast is served in an annexe in the adjoining side street, where a number of bedrooms are also located.
Nearby San Zaccaria; Piazza San Marco.

Riva degli Schiavoni, Castello 4182, 30122 Venezia **Tel** (041) 5224324 **Fax** (041) 5239267 **Location** between Sott. Calle San Zaccaria and Rio dei Greci; **vaporetto** San Zaccaria **Meals** breakfast **Prices** rooms L140,000–L230,000; standard double L180,000–L230,000; breakfast included **Rooms** 22; 20 double and twin, triple and family, 16 with bath or shower; 2 single, one with shower; all rooms have phone, TV, air-conditioning, safe **Facilities** sitting area, breakfast room **Credit cards** AE, MC, V **Children** accepted **Disabled** one room on ground floor **Pets** not accepted **Closed** never **Proprietors** Francesco and Giorgio Paganelli

Town guest-house

Pensione Wildner

Two long-standing budget options tucked between the four-star palaces along the Riva degli Schiavoni are the Paganelli (see above) and the Pensione Wildner. The same family has run the Wildner for over 35 years, maintaining an air of solid respectability amid the hubbub of the waterfront. All the bedrooms are similar in their old-fashioned simplicity, but the ones to try for are those with a view across the lagoon which are no more expensive than the rest. Some can sleep four, which makes a useful option for families or friends on a budget.
Nearby San Zaccaria; Piazza San Marco; San Giovanni in Bragora.

Riva degli Schiavoni, Castello 4161, 30122 Venezia **Tel** (041) 5227463 **Fax** (041) 5265615 **Location** on the waterfront between Ponte del Vin and Ponte dei Greci, close to Piazza San Marco **vaporetto** San Zaccaria, San Marco **Meals** breakfast, lunch, dinner **Prices** rooms L150,000–L370,000; standard double L220,000–L260,000; breakfast included; dinner from L30,000 **Rooms** 16 double and twin, triple or family with shower; all rooms have phone, TV, air-conditioning, safe **Facilities** breakfast room, bar, restaurant **Credit cards** AE, DC, MC, V **Children** accepted **Disabled** not suitable **Pets** accepted **Closed** never **Proprietor** Nicola Fullin

Castello

Town-house apartments

San Simeon

A nondescript door in an alley just off the mighty Riva degli Schiavoni leads to these three thoughtfully decorated one-bedroom apartments, perfect for a romantic twosome. (For families, an extra sofa bed in each could accommodate one or two small children.) The apartments, opened in 1996, belong to the Ai Due Fanali hotel (see page 45), and there is a direct line to the hotel if you need information or help. Two apartments enjoy fabulous views across the lagoon. Breakfast is provided each morning as well as maid service; dinner can also be shopped for and cooked at extra cost.

Nearby Piazza San Marco; Arsenale; San Giovanni in Bragora.

For information contact: Ai Due Fanali, Santa Croce 946, 30135 Venice **Tel** (041) 718490 **Fax** (041) 718344 **Location** off Riva degli Schiavoni between La Pietà and Ponte Ca' di Dio **vaporetto** Arsenale **Meals** breakfast, dinner on request **Prices** apartment without view L250,000–L350,000 per night; with view L280,000–L500,000 per night; breakfast included; minimum stay 4 nights **Rooms** 1 bedroom (double or twin bed), living area with sofa-bed, kitchen, bathroom **Facilities** maid service, cook available **Credit cards** AE, DC, MC, V **Children** accepted **Disabled** not suitable **Pets** not accepted **Closed** never **Proprietor** Marina Ferron

Dorsoduro

La Galleria

Through an improbable entrance next to a craft gallery, from which this unpretentious little hotel takes its name, we climbed a flight of steepish steps and travelled back some 80 years, for La Galleria appears frozen in the Edwardian era. Dark red flock paper covers the walls; floors are mostly plain wooden boards; the furniture is traditional Venetian – silk and gilt bedheads, large old-fashioned beds and chandeliers; and there are few amenities. No. 10 is the room to go for. Right on the Grand Canal, it sleeps four, has a glorious painted ceiling and only costs L20,000 more than a standard double.

Nearby Accademia gallery; Grand Canal.

Accademia, Dorsoduro 878/a, 30123 Venezia **Tel** (041) 5204172/5285814 **Fax** (041) 5204172 **Location** at NE corner of Campo della Carità, next to the Accademia bridge; **vaporetto** Accademia or water taxi **Meals** breakfast, served in room **Prices** rooms L75,000–L160,000; standard double

L140,000; breakfast included **Rooms** 10; 8 double and twin, 2 with bath; 1 single; 1 family with bath; all rooms have phone **Facilities** sitting area **Credit cards** not accepted **Children** accepted **Disabled** not suitable **Pets** accepted **Closed** 2–3 weeks in winter **Proprietor** Signor Benedetti

Locanda Montin

In the same family for generations, this *antica locanda* used to attract a devoted following among the glitteratti from Ezra Pound to Jimmy Carter. Fame was assured when the pergola-shaded garden became the setting for a scene in a film featuring Tony Musante and Florinda Bolkan, *Anonimo Veneziano*. Although it still has charisma, with paintings jostling for space on the walls, the restaurant is living off its reputation, serving ordinary food at highish prices. Bedrooms are basic, but lead off a magnificent beamed landing, furnished with ornate pieces and a wrought-iron chandelier.

Nearby Carmini; San Trovaso; Accademia gallery; Zattere.

San Trovaso, Fondamenta di Borgo, Dorsoduro 1147, Venezia **Tel** (041) 5227151 **Fax** (041) 5200255 **Location** just S of Calle Eremite; **vaporetto** Accademia, Ca' Rezzonico or water taxi **Meals** breakfast, lunch, dinner **Prices** rooms L55,000–L90,000; standard double L90,000; breakfast L7,000; menus from L50,000

Rooms 8; 3 double and twin, 3 triple, 1 family, 3 with shower, 4 with basin; one single with basin **Facilities** sitting area, restaurant, garden **Credit cards** AE, DC, MC, V **Children** accepted **Disabled** not suitable **Pets** accepted **Closed** 10 days Aug, 2–3 weeks Jan **Proprietor** Giuliamo Carretin

Dorsoduro

Apartments in private house

Palazzetto da Schio

Fondamenta Soranzo is a tranquil backwater lined with attractive houses, including this red-painted *palazzetto*, home of the da Schio family for the past 300 years. The present incumbent, Contessa da Schio, lives on the ground floor and *piano nobile*, while other parts of the house have been converted into three charming and comfortable apartments, available for any period of time from two days to six months. They are largely furnished with family antiques, including pictures and mirrors, and there are modern bits and pieces to fill in the gaps. Maid service available; references essential.

Nearby Santa Maria della Salute; Accademia; Zattere.

Fondamenta Soranzo, Dorsoduro 316/b, 30123 Venezia **Tel** (041) 5237937 **Fax** (041) 5237937 **Location** on canal between Grand and Giudecca Canals; **vaporetto** Salute or water taxi **Meals** breakfast **Prices** two-bedroom L320,000 per night; one-bedroom L250,000 per night; weekly rates available; service extra **Rooms** 3 apartments, 1 with 1 bedroom, 2 with 2 bedrooms; all with kitchen and bathroom; phone, heating **Facilities** maid service **Credit cards** AE, MC, V **Children** accepted if well-behaved **Disabled** not suitable **Pets** not accepted **Closed** never **Proprietor** Contessa Anna da Schio

Cannaregio

Town hotel

Abbazia

If you haven't guessed its origins from the name, then the interior is sure to provide a clue. High-ceilinged corridors are peppered with doors to almost monastic bedrooms. The former abbey's refectory has been converted to a sitting room of vast proportions, with wood panelling, a stunning stone floor and perfectly preserved pulpit jutting out from one wall. Even the welcoming staff don't quite succeed in overcoming the feeling of austerity. We recommend bedrooms 302 and 303, both spacious with huge windows and walk-in cupboards. Best of all is the delightful mature garden.

Nearby station; Scalzi; Palazzo Labia; San Geremia.

Calle Priuli, Cannaregio 68, 30121 Venezia
Tel (041) 717333
Fax (041) 717949
Location just E of the station; **vaporetto** Ferrovia
Meals breakfast
Prices rooms L85,000–L350,000; standard double L140,000–L350,000; breakfast included **Rooms** 39 double and twin, triple and family, all with bath or shower; all rooms have phone, TV, air-conditioning, minibar, hairdrier
Facilities bar/sitting room, breakfast room, garden
Credit cards AE, DC, MC, V
Children accepted **Disabled** no special facilities **Pets** not accepted **Closed** never
Manager Franco De Rossi

Town guest-house

Bernardi-Semenzato

Tucked away in a backstreet off the busy Strada Nova, this popular, reasonably priced hotel is handy for a visit to the church of Santi Apostoli, with its wonderful Tiepolo altarpiece. The Bernardi is a friendly, if eclectic place. Low beamed ceilings characterize the small ground floor, devoted to two breakfast rooms and dominated by a *trompe l'oeil* window, in which two children and a cat enjoy a fantasy view of Venice. Furnishings are modern and unfussy, bedrooms, modest; though one double room in a nearby annexe is decked out in a very different, over-the-top rococo style.

Nearby Ca' d'Oro; Santi Apostoli; Miracoli.

Calle dell' Oca, Santi Apostoli, Cannaregio 4366, 30121 Venezia
Tel (041) 5227257
Fax (041) 5222424
Location off NW corner of Campo Santi Apostoli; **vaporetto** Ca' d'Oro
Meals breakfast
Prices rooms L40,000–L110,000; standard double L100,000–L110,000; breakfast L5,000 **Rooms** 16; 13 double and twin (1 in annexe), 10 with shower; 3 single; all rooms have phone, TV (on request), safe
Facilities breakfast area and room **Credit cards** not accepted
Children accepted **Disabled** not suitable **Pets** accepted **Closed** 2–3 weeks Jan **Proprietor** Leonardo Biasin

Lagoon Islands

Resort hotel, Giudecca

Cipriani

We have heard differing opinions about the world-famous Cipriani and its two suite annexes with butler service, Palazzo Vendramin and the new Palazzetto. Our own view is that it is astonishingly overpriced, but if you are happy to accept that, then you can relax and enjoy its principal assets: the peaceful location and fabulous pool. On the subject of which, one recent visitor told us: 'On a hot day we went for lunch, for which we were content to pay a great deal, then asked if our young daughter could swim in the deserted pool. We were told she could not – house rules. We returned gratefully to the Gritti.'
Nearby Il Redentore church; Venice; Lagoon Islands.

Giudecca 10, 30133 Venezia **Tel** (041) 5207744 **Fax** (041) 5207745 **Location** 5 mins from San Marco by launch; **vaporetto** 24-hr hotel launch **Meals** breakfast, lunch, dinner **Prices** rooms L650,000–L4,100,000; standard double L900,000–L1,300,000; breakfast included; dinner from L130,000 **Rooms** 99; 59 double and twin, 7 single, 33 suites, all with bath; all rooms have phone, TV, air-conditioning, hairdrier, safe **Facilities** sitting rooms, dining rooms, bar, sauna, gym, lift, swimming pool, tennis court **Credit cards** AE, DC, MC, V **Children** accepted **Disabled** access possible **Pets** accepted **Closed** never **Manager** Natale Rusconi

Town hotel, Lido

Hungaria

Included for its novelty value, this hotel is a time-warp. Built in 1903 when the Lido was becoming all the fashion, its original name – Ansonia Palace – is still emblazoned across the imposing façade. Inside, little has changed, except that it is no longer grand; sweeping skirts and liveried staff have given way to shorts and backpacks. Downstairs, the public rooms are enormous though sparsely furnished, whilst, amazingly, the plain Edwardian furniture in the spacious bedrooms has been in place since 1906. Only the mattresses and the tiled bathrooms are more recent. Keenly priced, we felt.
Nearby Venice; Lagoon Islands.

Gran Viale Santa Maria Elisabetta 28, Lido, 30126 Venezia **Tel** (041) 5261212 **Fax** (041) 5267619 **Location** midway along Lido's main street; **vaporetto** Santa Maria Elisabetta **Meals** breakfast, lunch, dinner **Prices** rooms L70,000–L280,000; standard double L140,000–L280,000; breakfast included **Rooms** 70 double and single, 50 with bath or shower, 20 with washbasin only; all rooms have phone, TV, air-conditioning **Facilities** sitting room, dining room, lift, terrace, private parking **Credit cards** AE, DC, MC, V **Children** accepted **Disabled** access difficult **Pets** accepted **Closed** Dec to Feb **Managers** Flavio and Katarina Carraro

Lagoon Islands

Town hotel, Lido

La Meridiana

Although not right on the beach, La Meridiana has the sedate and quite agreeably old-fashioned air of a seaside hotel, which was purpose-built in the 1930s in rustic style, and where little seems to have changed since. Venetian marble floors and dark three-quarters panelled walls keep the ground floor refreshingly cool in summer. In winter, it has a more noticeably antiquated feel. In the main building, bedrooms are large and recently decorated. Numerous casement windows make them light and airy, and some have French doors on to a terrace. There are also nine rooms in a connecting annexe.

Nearby Venice; Lagoon Islands.

Via Lepanto 45, Lido, 30126 Venezia
Tel (041) 5260343
Fax (041) 5269240
Location at junction with Via Marcello; **vaporetto** San Nicolò
Meals breakfast
Prices rooms L70,000–L300,000; standard double L130,000–L300,000; breakfast included **Rooms** 34; 32 double and twin, with bath or shower; 2 single with shower; all rooms have phone, TV, air-conditioning, minibar, hairdrier, safe **Facilities** sitting room, bar, breakfast room, lift, garden, **Credit cards** AE, DC, MC, V **Children** accepted **Disabled** access possible **Pets** accepted **Closed** mid-Nov to Carnival **Proprietor** Gianluca Regazzo

Town hotel, Lido

Villa Parco

Set back from the road, through wrought-iron gates, in a romantic, if overgrown garden full of poplars, oleanders and statuary, this 19thC villa still looks impressive despite its now peeling paint. The area is a quiet residential one, a few minutes' walk from the waterfront. The villa itself is in the art nouveau style, though furnishings are mainly modern. Airy bedrooms are 'clean and comfortable', according to a recent report which also commends the 'helpful staff'. Breakfast is served in a small room in the basement or, from May to September, under a canopy in the pretty garden.

Nearby Venice; Lagoon Islands.

Via Rodi 1, Lido, 30126 Venezia
Tel (041) 5260015/5261495
Fax (041) 5267620
Location at junction with Via Modone e Corone and Via D. Selvo; **vaporetto** San Nicolò
Meals breakfast, snacks
Prices rooms L55,000–L280,000; standard double L85,000–L280,000; breakfast included **Rooms** 22; 21 double and twin, triple and family, all with bath or shower; 1 single with shower; all rooms have phone, TV, air-conditioning, minibar **Facilities** sitting area, breakfast room, garden, sun terrace, parking **Credit cards** AE, DC, MC, V **Children** accepted **Disabled** not suitable **Pets** accepted **Closed** never **Manager** Lea Zollino

Veneto

Town hotel, Asolo

Duse

The name was inspired by one of Asolo's best-known residents, the actress and mistress of D'Annunzio, Eleanor Duse. The cosier little sister of the Al Sole (see page 68) is decked out almost entirely in blue and yellow, with a spiral staircase and a tiny first-floor breakfast room. Dark wood furniture, striped curtains and blue bedspreads furnish all the bedrooms, with matching picture bows and fabric-covered lights, too twee for our taste. The best rooms are the doubles at the front, which include somewhere to sit, but pack your earplugs to block out the nearby Duomo's early matins bell.

Nearby Palladian villas; Possagno (10 km).

Via R. Browning 190, 31011 Asolo, Treviso
Tel (0423) 55241
Fax (0423) 5206554
Location off SE corner of Piazza Maggiore; parking in Piazza Maggiore
Meals breakfast **Prices** rooms L100,000–L250,000; standard double L200,000–L250,000; breakfast included **Rooms** 14; 8 double and twin, all with bath; 5 single with shower; 1 suite with bath; all rooms have phone, TV, air-conditioning, minibar **Facilities** breakfast room, meeting room, lift **Credit cards** AE, MC, V **Children** accepted **Disabled** access difficult **Pets** accepted **Closed** sometimes 2–3 weeks in Nov **Proprietor** Elena de Checchi

Town hotel, Castelfranco Veneto

Al Moretto

Admirers of that enigmatic artist, Giorgione, will not want to bypass Castelfranco Veneto, his birthplace. Within the moated Castello, its medieval core, you will find the Duomo and his *Madonna and Child* – flawed and damaged, yet magical.

Al Moretto, despite its modern appearance, is the oldest hostelry in town, in the same ownership for generations. Recently it has been completely refurbished, tastefully enough, but in a way that swaps character for streamlined comfort. You can be assured of a good night's rest in a well-equipped, softly coloured room, and a generous buffet breakfast.

Nearby Castello; Duomo; Casa del Giorgione.

Via San Pio X 10, 31033 Castelfranco Veneto, Treviso
Tel (0423) 721313
Fax (0423) 721066
Location outside the Castello, but in town centre, just off Mercato on road to Asolo; private parking
Meals breakfast **Prices** rooms L110,00–L140,000; standard double L140,000; breakfast L18,000 **Rooms** 34 single, double and twin, all with bath or shower; all rooms have phone, TV, air-conditioning, minibar, hairdrier, safe, lift **Facilities** sitting room, breakfast room, bar, garden **Credit cards** AE, DC, MC, V **Children** accepted **Disabled** access difficult **Pets** accepted **Closed** never **Proprietor** Signor Rigato

Veneto

Town inn, Cavaso del Tomba

Locanda Alla Posta

Cavaso del Tomba is a straggling village close to Possagno, birth-place of Canova and site of his moving Gipsoteca (gallery of plaster models) and his bizarre Temple. Alla Posta is a handsome building with something of the air of a Wild West saloon about it. There's a bar where locals congregate, and a simple restaurant in which surprisingly sophisticated food is served. Upstairs, wide, smartly decorated landings lead to the bedrooms, which are plain, but light, spacious and good value. Some are modern and functional, others – Nos 4 and 6 – have more interest, with matching Liberty furniture.
Nearby Possagno (2 km); Asolo (10 km).

Piazza XIII Martiri 13, 31034 Cavaso del Tomba, Treviso
Tel (0423) 543112
Location in town centre, 6 km W of SS348 at Pederobba
Meals breakfast, lunch, dinner
Prices double L80,000; breakfast included; dinner from L30,000
Rooms 7; 5 double and twin, 2 family, all with shower; all rooms have phone, TV
Facilities dining room, bar
Credit cards MC, V
Children accepted
Disabled not suitable
Pets accepted
Closed 1–15 July; restaurant closed Tues, Wed eve
Proprietor Remo Visentin

Town hotel, Conegliano

Canon d'Oro

Standing above the Veneto plain, Conegliano is a commercial and industrial centre, and the birthplace of Cima, painter of radiant Venetian Renaissance altarpieces. Arcaded Via XX Settembre is lined with handsome mansions, one of which is this 16thC building. However, the hotel's frescoed exterior is the last you will see of the past: the interior is bland, with no original features and tired, functional public rooms. Bedrooms are better: Nos 305 and 306 under the eaves have most appeal. There is a flower-filled terraced garden, and despite its shortcomings, this is the best bet for a bed in Conegliano.
Nearby Treviso (28 km); Belluno (54 km).

Via XX Settembre 129, 31015 Conegliano, Treviso
Tel (0438) 34246
Fax (0438) 34246
Location in the heart of the old town, with parking
Meals breakfast
Prices rooms L80,000– L135,000; standard double L135,000; breakfast L12,000
Rooms 35 double and twin and single, 1 with bath, 34 with shower; all rooms have phone, TV, air-conditioning, minibar, hairdrier **Facilities** sitting room, breakfast room, garden, lift
Credit cards AE, DC, MC, V
Children accepted **Disabled** access difficult **Pets** not accepted **Closed** never
Proprietors Giancarlo and Piero Capraro

Veneto

Country villa, Dolo

Villa Ducale

When we visited this grand 19thC villa hotel, in a formal garden filled with statues, the marble-floored reception and vast chandeliered dining hall were seething with management consultants attending a reception. Not an uncommon event, since it has conference facilities for up to 200 people. Though recently restored, much of the original decoration looks dowdy, as it must have from the outset. Neutral colours predominate and, despite 19thC murals and decorative parquet floors, bedrooms have a shuttered-up feel. There is an apartment (No. 22) ideal for a family of five.

Nearby Palladian villas; Riviera del Brenta.

Riviera Martiri della Libertà 75, 30031 Dolo, Venezia **Tel/Fax** (041) 5608020/5608004 **Location** 2 km E of Dolo, on the SS11; in own grounds with ample parking **Meals** breakfast, lunch, dinner **Prices** rooms L160,000–L280,000; standard double L220,000–L260,000; breakfast included **Rooms** 11; 6 double and twin, 3 triple, 2 family, all with bath or shower; all rooms have phone, TV, air-conditioning, minibar, hairdrier, safe **Facilities** breakfast room, sitting room, dining room, meeting room, bar, restaurant, garden **Credit cards** AE, DC, MC, V **Children** accepted **Disabled** ground-floor room **Pets** accepted **Closed** never **Manager** Marco Fogarin

Country villa, Gorgo al Monticano

Villa Revedin

In open countryside just outside the little town of Gorgo al Monticano, Villa Revedin is sheltered within its own mature park. As the original structure of the 15thC villa remains intact, the mostly modern furnishings tend to jar – for instance, the bright chairs and contemporary mural in the classical entrance. Our inspector was impressed by the vast reading room with its marble floor and frescoed ceiling, but couldn't imagine curling up in here with a book. The rustic restaurant specializes in fish and looks as if it should be by the sea. As you go in, there's a long counter groaning with fresh fish on ice.

Nearby Treviso (32 km); Venice within reach.

Via Palazzi 4, Gorgo al Monticano, 31040 Oderzo, Treviso **Tel/Fax** (0422) 800033 **Location** 4 km NE of Oderzo; in own grounds; parking **Meals** breakfast, lunch, dinner **Prices** rooms L97,000–L194,000; standard double L172,000; breakfast L14,000; dinner from L50,000 **Rooms** 32; 14 double and twin, 14 single, 4 suites, all with bath or shower; all rooms have phone, TV, air-conditioning, minibar, hairdrier **Facilities** breakfast room, sitting room, bar, restaurant **Credit cards** AE, DC, MC, V **Children** accepted **Disabled** not suitable **Pets** not accepted **Closed** restaurant Sun dinner, Mon, Jan, 10 days Aug **Manager** Stefano Bison

Veneto

Town hotel, Mogliano Veneto

Villa Stucky

In its own wood-fringed garden, Villa Stucky is an imposing 19thC building whose mid-European flavour can be traced to the Swiss Family Stucky who built it after demolishing a classical villa. Today it is favoured by business guests and conference organizers. The formality of the high-ceilinged public rooms is carried through to the bedrooms and suites, which have grandiose names – 'Principessa Sissi', 'Regina Margherita' – and decoration to match. Although under the old timbered roof, 'Estasi' and 'Venezia' are more modern in style. There's no shortage of space, even in standard doubles.
Nearby Venice (14 km); Treviso (10 km); Padua (30 km).

Via Don Bosco 47, 31021 Mogliano Veneto, Treviso **Tel** (041) 5904528 **Fax** (041) 5904566 **Location** in town centre; in grounds with parking **Meals** breakfast, lunch, dinner **Prices** rooms L185,000–L350,000; standard double L300,000; breakfast included; dinner from L50,000 **Rooms** 20; 11 double and twin, 5 single, 4 junior suites all with bath or shower; all rooms have phone, TV, fax/modem point, air-conditioning, minibar, hair-drier, safe **Facilities** sitting area, dining room, bar, lift, garden **Credit cards** AE, DC, MC, V **Children** accepted **Disabled** no special facilities **Pets** not accepted **Closed** 2 weeks in Aug **Manager** Antonio Pianura

Restaurant-with-rooms, Montagnana

Aldo Moro

Montagnana is one of the most attractive towns in the Veneto, its arcaded streets enclosed by a superb rectangle of moated medieval walls. The Aldo Moro, opened in 1940 by the present owner's father (not the assassinated politician) makes the best base for an overnight stay. Bedrooms are a rather jarring mix of old and new, featuring glossy black headboards and wardrobes, and in each, a startlingly bright red armchair. Some bathrooms are large, with inviting showers properly enclosed. The restaurant rambles over several rooms, gleaming with polished glass and carefully folded napery.
Nearby Villa Pisani; Este (15 km); Padua (49 km).

Via Marconi 27, 35044 Montagnana, Padova **Tel** (0429) 81351 **Fax** (0429) 82842 **Location** in town centre; parking in hotel garage or in street **Meals** breakfast, lunch, dinner **Prices** rooms L95,000–L185,000; standard double L145,000; breakfast L13,000 **Rooms** 25; 20 double and twin, 5 suites, all with shower; all rooms have phone, TV, air-conditioning; minibar in suites **Facilities** restaurant, breakfast room, sitting area, bar, meeting room, small garden **Credit cards** AE, DC, MC, V **Children** accepted **Disabled** not suitable **Pets** accepted **Closed** 2 weeks in Jan, 2 weeks in Aug; restaurant closed Mon **Proprietor** Sergio Moro

Veneto

Town hotel, Padua

Leon Bianco

'Charming' may not be quite the right word for this modern
hotel, with its plate-glass doors and smooth contemporary furnishings. But it has a certain – if somewhat self-conscious – style,
and a great position overlooking the famous Caffè Pedrocchi.
To be avoided by the prudish though – a screen decorated with
an explicit nude mural dominates the small green sitting room.
Bedrooms are remarkably large with parquet floors, white formi-
ca furniture and framed American posters. Summer guests are
served breakfast beneath calico parasols on a roof terrace lined
with plants in terracotta pots.
Nearby Palazzo della Ragione; Scrovegni Chapel; Il Santo.

Piazzetta Pedrocchi 12,
35122 Padova
Tel (049) 8750814
Fax (049) 8756184
Location opposite Caffè
Pedrocchi, just E of Piazza delle
Erbe; garage parking
Meals breakfast
Prices rooms L121,000 –
L211,000; standard double
L151,000; breakfast L15,000

Rooms 22; 20 double and twin,
triple and family, 4 with bath,
16 with shower; 2 single with
shower; all rooms have phone,
TV, air-conditioning, minibar
Facilities breakfast room, sitting
area, lift, roof terrace **Credit
cards** AE, DC, MC, V **Children**
accepted **Disabled** access
difficult **Pets** accepted **Closed**
never **Manager** Paulo Morosi

Town hotel, Padua

Majestic Toscanelli

The hotel is neither majestic nor Tuscan but it does occupy an
unusually quiet spot in the heart of old Padua, with a welcome
splash of flowers and greenery in the little square outside.
Though the Toscanelli has long appeared in our all-Italy guide,
a night's stay persuaded us that it was nothing very special, and
we were somewhat baffled to know why it was classed as a four
star. Bedrooms, whether described as 'Venetian', 'Louis-
Philippe' or '19thC English', are run-of-the-mill, and in our
case, hard pillows and a plastic-curtained shower which flooded
the bathroom did not seem up to scratch.
Nearby Palazzo della Ragione; Scrovegni Chapel; Il Santo.

Via dell' Arco 2, 35122 Padova
Tel (049) 663244 **Fax** (049)
8760025 **Location** town centre,
near Piazza delle Erbe; by car
follow signs for Zona Sud, then
pick up helpful hotel signs;
parking **Meals** breakfast **Prices**
rooms L150,000–L330,000;
standard double L195,000–
L280,000; breakfast included
Rooms 32; 26 double and twin,

3 superior double and twin; 3
suites, all with bath or shower;
all rooms have phone, TV, air-
conditioning, minibar,
hairdrier; safe in some rooms
Facilities breakfast room, sitting
room, bar, lift **Credit cards** AE,
DC, MC, V **Children** accepted
Disabled access possible **Pets**
accepted **Closed** never
Proprietor Anna-Maria Morosi

Veneto

Azienda Agrituristica, Pozzolo

Valle Verde

In a lush, peaceful valley, this cream-painted house offers five modest bedrooms with modern facilities, but its *raison d'être* is a bustling restaurant with a vast terrace for *al fresco* meals. There is no menu, but *mamma* – Evelina – does all the cooking herself, producing what she feels like and does best: pasta, roast meat – simple country fare. The restaurant is furnished with rush-seated chairs; immaculate linen covers the tables. Huge arched glass doors open on to the terrace, beyond which is a playground where children can slide and swing amidst the vines. This *agriturismo* is a cut above the norm.
Nearby Palladian villas; Vicenza (24 km).

Via Fagnini 13, 36020 Pozzolo di Villaga, Vicenza
Tel (0444) 868242/868586
Location from Arcugnano, take right turn to Barbarano, signed Pozzolo, then keep left for Valverde; ample parking
Meals breakfast, lunch, dinner
Prices rooms L40,000 per person; half board L60,000; full board L70,000; breakfast included **Rooms** 5; 1 twin, 1 triple, 2 family, all with shower; 1 single with bath; all rooms have phone, TV (on request)
Facilities restaurant, garden
Credit cards not accepted
Children welcome
Disabled access difficult
Pets not accepted
Closed restaurant Mon
Proprietors Donello family

Chalet guest-house, Tai di Cadore

Villa Marinotti

Tai di Cadore lies just along the road from Pieve di Cadore, birthplace of Titian and the main town in this mountainous and thickly wooded region, and Villa Marinotti has a typical backdrop of dark forest and rocky peaks.

The owners of the modern stone, wood and white-painted chalet, open only in summer, have created five spacious and comfortable suites, each one with its own little sitting room, sleeping up to four people. There is a dining room serving good home cooking, and in the expansive grounds are a sauna and tennis court.
Nearby Pieve di Cadore (1.5 km); Cortina d'Ampezzo (30 km).

Via Manzago 21, 32040 Tai di Cadore, Belluno
Tel (0435) 32231
Fax (0435) 33335
Location in village, on SS51 Cortina to Pieve di Cadore road (1.5 km SE of Pieve); ample parking **Meals** breakfast, dinner
Prices rooms L110,000–L250,000; suite for two L160,000–L180,000; breakfast included; dinner from L30,000
Rooms 5 suites, all with bath; all rooms have phone, TV
Facilities sitting room, dining room, bar, meeting room, terrace **Credit cards** AE, MC, V
Children accepted **Disabled** access difficult **Pets** not accepted **Closed** Oct to Jun
Proprietors Laura and Giorgio Marinotti

Veneto

Country hotel, Torri del Benaco

Europa

The decoration in this 1950s villa is typical of the period: brown colour schemes, modern wood panelling, garish floor tiles. However, the friendly Casarottis have done their best to knock off some of the hard edges with fresh flowers, and to make what regular visitors call 'a happy, welcoming hotel'. Bright rugs rescue the sitting room from being too gloomy, and the dining room is airy and light, if a trifle banal. Bedrooms look more up-to-date, with colourful fabrics; seven have views of Lake Garda. The setting is pleasant and the pretty garden includes a shady terrace for breakfast or candlelit dinners.
Nearby Sirmione (38 km); Verona (45 km).

Via G. D'Annunzio 13–15, 37010 Torri del Benaco, Verona **Tel** (045) 7225086 **Fax** (045) 6296632 **Location** 150 m off main Gardesana road, just S of town; in own grounds with ample parking **Meals** breakfast, lunch, dinner **Prices** rooms L50,000–L166,000; standard double L134,000–L156,000; breakfast included; dinner from L40,000 **Rooms** 18; 17 double and twin, 7 with bath, 8 with shower; 1 single; all rooms have phone, hairdrier **Facilities** sitting room, bar, dining room, garden, swimming pool **Credit cards** MC, V **Children** accepted **Disabled** no special facilities **Pets** not accepted **Closed** mid-Oct to Easter **Proprietors** Casarotti family

---

Restaurant-with-rooms, Treviso

Alle Beccherie/Campeol

Alle Beccherie is an unpretentious family-run restaurant at the heart of old Treviso. 'Superb food without being overpriced,' says one recent visitor, while others praise the dignified, old-fashioned atmosphere of this fine old Venetian-style building. Across the street is the owner's Albergo Campeol, which has mostly large, plain rooms with big beds and modern furnishings, including roomy wardrobes. Our bathroom had a huge shower and cruelly effective mirror lighting, and the spacious bedroom had a canal view. Be prepared for a gruff and peremptory welcome from the non English-speaking *patron*.
Nearby Piazza dei Signori; Palazzo dei Trecento; Duomo.

Piazza Ancilotto 10, 31100 Treviso **Tel** (0422) 540871/56601 **Fax** (0422) 540871 **Location** city centre; parking in street, or in car park in Piazza del Duomo **Meals** breakfast, lunch, dinner **Prices** rooms single L80,000; double L110,000; breakfast L8,000; dinner from L50,000 **Rooms** 14 single, double and twin, all with shower; all rooms have phone, TV, hairdrier **Facilities** dining room, breakfast room **Credit cards** AE, DC, MC, V **Children** accepted **Disabled** not suitable **Closed** restaurant closed Sun eve, Mon, Aug **Proprietor** Signor Campeol

Veneto

Agriturismo, Valdobbiadene

Riva de Milàn

As we were shown around this ranch-style *agriturismo* by Signora Bernardi, an elderly woman who only speaks Italian, we were struck by how rustic this place is. Although the locality is almost suburban, the cream house with wooden shutters and doors and a large veranda is on a working farm, where they breed peacocks as a sideline. As you'd expect, the cheerful restaurant offers morning-fresh produce and home cooking. Six simple rooms in contemporary country style nestle at the top of the house under a sloping beamed roof, with modern wood furniture and brand-new showers.

Nearby Asolo (26 km); Belluno (47 km); Treviso (36 km).

Via Erizzo 126, Valdobbiadene, Treviso	**Rooms** 6 double and twin, all with shower; all rooms have TV
Tel (0423) 973496/973030	**Facilities** restaurant
Location from Valdobbiadene, off road to Bigolino, past sign to Villa Nova and up unmarked track to right through vines; ample parking	**Credit cards** not accepted
	Children accepted
	Disabled access difficult
	Pets accepted
Meals breakfast, lunch, dinner	**Closed** restaurant Sep to Easter and Mon
Prices rooms: double L80,000; breakfast included	**Proprietors** Bernardi family

Agriturismo, Villorba

Podere del Convento

Close to the Relais El Toulà (see page 80), but at quite the other end of the scale, Podere del Convento is a working farm producing wine and fruit, an equestrian centre and a restaurant, with six attractive bedrooms also available. These have roughcast walls and ceilings open to the tiled roof, with large beds in bright yellow or peach, prettily upholstered bedroom chairs and the odd attractive piece of old country furniture. Bathrooms are tiled in primary colours. The rambling, busily decorated restaurant is homely and bustling, often packed with local families. No English is spoken.

Nearby Palladian villas; Treviso (5 km); Venice (40 km).

Via 1V Novembre 16, 31050 Villorba, Treviso	**Rooms** 6 double, all with shower; all rooms have phone
Tel (0422) 920044	**Facilities** dining room, bar; riding available
Fax (0422) 920044	
Location in Villorba, off the SS13, 5 km N of Treviso, set amid farmland	**Credit cards** AE, MC, V
	Children accepted
	Disabled not suitable
Meals breakfast, lunch, dinner	**Pets** not accepted
Prices rooms L45,000–L70,000; double L70,000; breakfast L5,000; dinner from L25,000	**Closed** Aug
	Proprietor Renzo Milani

Lombardia

Lakeside hotel, Limone sul Garda

Capo Reamol

Lake Garda is famous for its winds, and this relaxed and comfortable hotel (standing on a particularly breezy spot), provides some of the best facilities around, including a beefy German windsurfing instructor. Though the hotel lacks character, the unremarkable building enjoys a marvellous setting, and the activities on offer are numerous. The health and beauty team will try to eliminate your stress, using ayurvedic principles, or you could go for a punishing (or gentle) mountain bike ride. In the evening, you might find yourself dressing up in a toga for one of the hotel's regular Roman feasts.
Nearby Riva del Garda and ferries (11 km); Gardone (30 km).

25010 Limone sul Garda, Brescia **Tel** (0365) 954040 **Fax** (0365) 954262 **Location** just N of town on lakeside; in own grounds with ample parking **Meals** breakfast, lunch, dinner **Prices** rooms L138,000–L336,000; standard double L276,000; breakfast included; dinner from L60,000 **Rooms** 59; 56 double and twin, 3 with bath, 53 with shower; 3 single with shower; all rooms have phone, TV, minibar, hairdrier **Facilities** restaurant, bar, sauna, fitness/beauty centre, terraces, swimming pool, beach **Credit cards** not accepted **Children** welcome **Disabled** specially adapted rooms available **Pets** not accepted **Closed** mid-Oct to May **Proprietor** Angelica Glas

Lakeside villa, Sirmione

Villa Cortine Palace

The setting of this luxury headland hotel, a many-columned neoclassical villa, is memorable. From the charming streets of Sirmione, vast iron gates admit you to a private drive which sweeps past elaborate fountains and statues set in magnificent exotic gardens. Inside the late-19thC villa are a series of frescoed and highly ornamented public rooms and five elegant bedrooms. The rest of the suitably well-appointed bedrooms, all with lake-facing balconies, are in the grim 1950s extension, which is as banal as the villa is grandiose. To sum up: hardly charming and small, but special, with unmissable grounds.
Nearby Lake Garda; Brescia (39 km); Verona (35 km).

Via Grotte 6, 25019 Sirmione, Brescia **Tel** (030) 9905890 **Fax** (030) 916390 **Location** 1 km beyond Sirmione; ample parking **Meals** breakfast, lunch, dinner **Prices** rooms L460,000–L1050,000; standard double L460,000–L590,000; breakfast included; dinner from L80,000 **Rooms** 49; 43 twin, 2 suites, 4 junior suites, all with bath; all rooms have phone, TV, air-conditioning, minibar, hairdrier **Facilities** sitting rooms, dining rooms, bar, lift, gardens, terraces, swimming pool, tennis court, private beach **Credit cards** AE, DC, MC, V **Children** accepted **Disabled** no special facilities **Pets** accepted **Closed** Nov to Apr **Manager** Roberto Cappelletto

Trentino-Alto Adige

Country hotel, Alberé di Tenna

Margherita

In a pine forest on a mountainside, this family-run hotel could hardly have a more peaceful setting. Although peace is of the essence (a sign requests you to avoid 'unnecessary noise'), families are positively encouraged. One swimming pool is specifically for children, with a playground reassuringly close to the sunloungers, and two spacious apartments are ideal for families. A modern chalet, it has a lovely big terrace at the front, but uninspired decoration inside. Public rooms are airy but characterless. The original 1950s bedrooms tend to be small and dreary, so ask for one of the larger new rooms.

Nearby Trento (21 km); Lago di Caldonazzo (5 km).

Località Pineta Alberé 2, 38050 Tenna, Trento **Tel** (0461) 706445/706045 **Fax** (0461) 707854 **Location** NE of Tenna; in own grounds with ample parking **Meals** breakfast, lunch, dinner **Prices** rooms L68,000–L90,000; standard double L50,000–L80,000; breakfast included; dinner from L30,000 **Rooms** 52; 41 double and twin, 8 single, 3 family, all with bath or shower; all rooms have phone, TV, hairdrier **Facilities** sitting/games room, dining room, meeting room, bar, garden, swimming pool, tennis court **Credit cards** AE, MC, V **Children** welcome **Disabled** no special facilities **Pets** accepted **Closed** Nov to Feb **Proprietor** Lino Angeli

Country castle, Appiano Monte

Schloss Freudenstein

Set amidst vines and fruit trees, this 800-year-old castle enjoys wonderful views. The building is imposing, rather sombre and beginning to crumble ... but not without atmosphere. There is a romantic inner courtyard, with stone arches and ancient uneven flagstones, and you can dine on the *loggia* which runs alongside. Beyond, amongst a series of rather ghostly rooms, a vast frescoed hall acts as the sitting room, and there is a cosier bar. Bedrooms are either large or huge, comfortable but lacking in style. Our set-menu dinner was elegantly presented by the gracious proprietor. More guest house than hotel.

Nearby Bolzano (10 km); Lake Caldaro (10 km).

Via Masaccio 6, Appiano Monte 39057 Bolzano **Tel** (0471) 660638 **Fax** (0471) 660122 **Location** 10 km SW of Bolzano, in own grounds with ample parking **Meals** breakfast, dinner **Prices** half board L150,000–L180,000 per person **Rooms** 14 single, double and twin and family rooms, all with bath or shower; all rooms have phone, hairdrier, safe **Facilities** dining room, sitting room, courtyard, bar, garden, swimming pool **Credit cards** not accepted **Children** accepted **Disabled** not suitable **Pets** not accepted **Closed** mid-Nov to mid-Mar **Proprietor** Gisela Ehmer-Insam

Trentino-Alto Adige

Dominik

With its own fabulous swimming pool complex and the cable car
to the ski slopes just a ten-minute drive away, this comfortable,
modern Relais et Châteaux hotel makes a great base for the fitness conscious. Set in a garden of lawns and flower-filled terraces, it has an open-plan ground floor: a sitting room, with
large open hearth, comfy chairs and coffee tables piled high
with magazines, and two dining rooms – one in traditional style,
the other, contemporary. The local cuisine reveals
Mediterranean influences. Bedrooms are sunny with varied
colour schemes; the higher you go, the better the view.
Nearby Duomo; Bolzano (40 km).

Via Terzo di Sotto 13, 39042
Bressanone, Bolzano
Tel (0472) 830144 **Fax** (0472)
836554 **Location** on N side of
town; with garage **Meals**
breakfast, lunch, dinner **Prices**
rooms L110,000–L190,000;
standard double L110,000–
L120,000; breakfast included;
dinner from L60,000 **Rooms**
28; 18 double and twin, 9
single, 1 suite, all with bath or
shower; all rooms have phone,
TV, minibar, hairdrier, safe
Facilities sitting room, restaurant, bar, lift, indoor pool
complex **Credit cards** AE, DC,
MC, V **Children** accepted
Disabled no facilities **Pets**
accepted **Closed** Jan to Mar, 3
weeks in Nov **Proprietors**
Dominik Demetz family

Villa Madruzzo

This is an imposing, red and yellow villa in neoclassical style,
well placed for visiting Trento and set in lovely gardens – it is a
shame that traffic noise from the nearby main road permeates
the peace. Public rooms are pleasant, particularly the three dining rooms which are decorated along elegant, classical lines with
Venetian chandeliers and a few well-placed antique sideboards
and portraits. The spacious terrace running along two sides of
the house provides plenty of room for outdoor eating.
Bedrooms in the main villa have more character than those in
the rather banal extension.
Nearby Trento; Valsugana (10 km); Lake Caldonazzo (10 km).

Via Ponte Alto 26, 38050
Cognola di Trento, Trento
Tel (0461) 986220 **Fax** (0461)
986361 **Location** 3 km NE of
Trento; in grounds with
parking **Meals** breakfast, lunch,
dinner **Prices** rooms L100,000–
L160,000; standard double
L160,000; breakfast included;
dinner from L40,000 **Rooms**
51; 26 double and twin, 22
single, 3 triple, 4 with bath, 47
with shower; all rooms have
phone, TV, minibar, hairdrier,
safe **Facilities** restaurant, bar,
lift, terraces, garden **Credit
cards** AE, DC, MC, V **Children**
welcome **Disabled** ramps to
public rooms, bedrooms on
ground floor, wide lift **Pets**
accepted **Closed** restaurant Sun
Proprietor Signor Polonioli

Trentino-Alto Adige

Mountain chalet, Colfosco

Capella

The present owners are the fourth generation to manage the hotel, which was rebuilt in classic chalet style in the 1960s. Renata Pizzinini's grandfather, a famous guide who collected walkers from Brunico by horse, pioneered tourism in the area. The hotel is comfortable and welcoming, but a trifle cluttered and fabrics are over-patterned. Tables are packed into the dining room, and myriad burnished metal lights are suspended from the ornate panelled ceiling. You can enjoy an indoor pool, skiing or walking from the door and spectacular views. There are 17 rooms in the Tyrolean-style Residence next door.
Nearby Brunico (34 km); Corvara (0.5 km); Cortina (36 km).

39030 Colfosco, Bolzano **Tel** (0471) 836183 **Fax** (0471) 836561 **Location** on edge of village, W of Corvara; in garden with parking **Meals** breakfast, lunch, dinner **Prices** half board L110,000–L230,000 per person per day **Rooms** 40; 30 double and twin, 6 single, 2 with bath, 4 with shower; 4 suites, all with bath or shower; all rooms have phone, TV, minibar (on request), safe **Facilities** sitting room, bar, dining room, indoor swimming pool, sauna, solarium, gym, lift, terrace, garden **Credit cards** AE, DC, MC, V **Children** accepted **Disabled** no special facilities **Pets** accepted **Closed** Oct to mid-Dec, Apr to mid-June **Proprietor** Renata Pizzinini

---

Resort hotel, Corvara

La Perla

We include the four-star La Perla for those who are looking for a touch of luxury and plenty of facilities in their Dolomite hotel without losing too much character. Situated in the centre of Corvara, in the heart of the lovely Alpine region of Alta Badia, the hotel is extremely comfortable in 'sophisticated rustic' style and offers many services and facilities, from hairdressing to bowling, with a luxurious new health and beauty centre and an outdoor heated pool for summer. The restaurant, La Stuä de Michil, serves elegant dishes. The modern bedrooms lack the character of the many public rooms, but are well equipped.
Nearby Val Gardena; Cortina d'Ampezzo (36 km).

Via Centro 44, 39033 Corvara in Badia, Bolzano **Tel** (0471) 836133 **Fax** (0471) 836568 **Location** in town centre; ample parking **Meals** breakfast, lunch, dinner **Prices** rooms L130,000–L620,000; standard double L220,000–L520,000; breakfast included; dinner from L50,000 **Rooms** 52 double and twin, single and suites, all with bath; all rooms have phone, TV, hairdrier **Facilities** sitting rooms, dining rooms, games room, lift, terrace, indoor and outdoor swimming pool **Credit cards** AE, DC, MC, V **Children** welcome **Disabled** access possible **Pets** accepted **Closed** mid-Dec to mid-Apr, July to Sep **Proprietors** Costa family

Trentino-Alto Adige

<hr>

Country apartments, Fié allo Sciliar

Moarhof

This is an area where it is easy to find simple accommodation: every other house offers rooms or apartments for rent. This 12thC farmhouse building with a sundial painted on the front caught our eye as being special. Situated just above the village of Fié, there are eight apartments for between two and five people, and all are decorated in rustic Tyrolean farmhouse style. Several boast their original wood panelling and ceramic stoves; most have separate sitting and bedrooms, and well-equipped kitchen areas (with washing machine and dishwasher). There are two with balconies.

Nearby Bolzano (20 km); Castelrotto (10 km).

39050 Fié allo Sciliar, Bolzano
Tel/Fax (0471) 725095
Location 20 km E of Bolzano, outside village; in own garden with ample parking
Meals none
Prices rooms L70,000–L105,000 per person per day
Rooms 8 apartments; all apartments have kitchen, bathroom, TV (on request)
Facilities table tennis, garden, swimming pool, barbecue
Credit cards not accepted
Children welcome
Disabled not suitable
Pets accepted
Closed never
Proprietors Kompatscher family

<hr>

Mountain hotel, La Villa

La Villa

If you want to stay in the lovely Alta Badia region of the Dolomites, here is a simpler alternative to La Perla in Corvara (see page 145). Unfortunately we were unable to send an inspector as the hotel was closed at the time, but we include it on the strength of a letter of recommendation, which praises its beautiful and peaceful setting on the slope of a hillside with wide views across the valley. 'An old mountain building completely renovated, with a garden full of flowers in summer. Inside the hotel is fresh and neat, with lots of white walls, natural fabrics and modern pine furniture.'

Nearby Corvara (4.5 km); Cortina d'Ampezzo (35 km).

La Villa, 39030 Alta Badia, Bolzano
Tel (0471) 847035
Fax (0471) 847393
Location off SS244 Corvara to Brunico road, 4.5 km N of Corvara; with parking **Meals** breakfast, lunch, dinner **Prices** rooms L80,000–L260,000; breakfast included; dinner from L35,000 **Rooms** 27 double, twin and single, all with bath or shower; all rooms have phone, TV, hairdrier **Facilities** sitting room, dining room, lift, sauna/fitness room terrace, garden **Credit cards** MC, V **Children** welcome **Disabled** access difficult **Pets** not accepted **Closed** mid-Apr to mid-June and mid-Sep to Dec **Manager** Mariangela Pizzinini

Trentino-Alto Adige

Medieval manor, Merano

Castel Rundegg

A recent reporter wrote about this hotel, '... a lovely old building, but it's a pity it doesn't enjoy a more rural setting. It's on quite a busy road with other buildings close by.' She found Castel Rundegg, 'a bit too slick and very beauty farm orientated'. The health and beauty complex is certainly impressive, and guests can submit themselves to all the latest treatments. The restaurant has a cellar-like atmosphere, with its stone-vaulted ceiling and alcove rooms. Bedrooms are well-appointed with luxurious bathrooms and special features. One of the most sought-after, the turret room, commands a 360-degree view.
Nearby Passirio river; Passirio valley.

Via Scena 2, 39012 Merano, Bolzano **Tel** (0473) 234100 **Fax** (0473) 237200 **Location** on E side of Merano; in own grounds with ample parking **Meals** breakfast, lunch, dinner **Prices** rooms L162,000–L496,000; breakfast included; dinner from L70,000 **Rooms** 29; 22 double and twin, 20 with bath, 2 with shower; 5 single with shower; 1 suite, 1 family, both with bath; all rooms have phone, TV, minibar, hairdrier, safe **Facilities** sitting room, bar, dining rooms, indoor swimming pool, sauna, health and beauty farm, lift, garden **Credit cards** AE, DC, MC, V **Children** accepted **Disabled** not suitable **Pets** accepted **Closed** never **Proprietors** Sinn family

---

Mountain guest-house, San Cipriano

Stefaner

High up in the beautiful Tires valley, this is a fairly new Tyrolean chalet whose wooden balconies are a riot of colour in summer (unfortunately views from the front are interrupted by a row of lofty trees). Inside, furnishings are modern and uniform, and the carpet is busily patterned, but warm colours and a roaring fire in cold weather impart a cosy atmosphere. The simply-furnished rooms all have balconies and, though some are small, are spotless. The young Villgrattners are warm hosts, and Giorgio is an excellent and creative cook – dinner is served on the stroke of seven. Great value for money.
Nearby Bolzano (17 km); Sciliar Natural Park (2 km); skiing.

San Cipriano, 39050 Tires, Bolzano **Tel/Fax** (0471)) 642175/ 642302 **Location** on main road in village, 17 km E of Bolzano, 3 km E of Tires; with parking **Meals** breakfast, dinner **Prices** half board L64,000–L90,000 per person **Rooms** 16; 14 double and twin, 2 with bath, 12 with shower; 2 single with shower; all rooms have phone, TV on request **Facilities** sitting room, dining room, bar, lift, garden **Credit cards** not accepted **Children** welcome **Disabled** access possible **Pets** not accepted **Closed** 5 Nov to 26 Dec, mid-Jan to Feb **Proprietors** Villgrattner family

Trentino-Alto Adige

Mountain guest-house, San Floriano

Obereggen

The setting for this modest chalet is ideal for skiers. At the top of a gorgeous Dolomite valley, 1,550 metres above sea level, it is only yards from lifts which give access to 40 kilometres of piste (one in use during summer). From the sunny terrace you can watch nearby sporting activity or the sun setting behind craggy peaks across the valley. The focal point of the hotel is the cosy bar with its ceramic stove, stags' heads and hunting trophies. The bedrooms are simple but clean with plump duvets adding a touch of comfort. About half have balconies, and those at the top enjoy fabulous views. Charming hostess; good food.
Nearby Bolzano (15 km); skiing at Latemar ski centre.

Via Obereggen 8, San Floriano (Obereggen), 39050 Nova Ponente, Bolzano
Tel (0471) 615722
Fax (0471) 615889
Location 17 km SE of Bolzano Nord motorway exit, 5 km off SS241; on edge of village with parking
Meals breakfast, dinner
Prices half board L58,000–

L70,000 per person
Rooms 12; 11 double (2 twin), 1 single, all with shower; all rooms have phone
Credit cards not accepted
Children welcome
Disabled access difficult
Pets accepted
Closed after Easter to June, mid-Oct to Dec
Proprietors Pichler family

Mountain chalet, Selva

Sporthotel Granvara

The name says it all. Facilities include a squash court, gym and indoor pool. For ski enthusiasts, it offers direct access to the Dolomite superski area via the Ciampinoi cable car, and at the end of the day, you can ski back to the door. If you need advice, the owner and his son are both instructors. Like many hotels in the area, it is a chalet, surrounded by pastures and glorious scenery, its wooden balconies brimming with geraniums in summer. Inside, the large comfortable Tyrolean-style public rooms are particularly inviting after a hard day on the slopes. Bedrooms are relatively anonymous.
Nearby Bolzano (40 km); Bressanone (35 km).

39048 Selva Gardena, Bolzano
Tel (0471) 795250
Fax (0471) 794336
Location 1 km E of Selva; in garden with parking and garage
Meals breakfast, lunch, dinner
Prices half board L125,000– L230,000 per person per day
Rooms 32; 20 double and twin, 2 single, 10 suites, all with bath or shower; all rooms have

phone, TV, hairdrier, safe
Facilities sitting rooms, bar, dining room, conference room, indoor swimming pool, sauna, squash court, gym, lift, garden
Credit cards AE, MC, V
Children accepted **Disabled** no special facilities **Pets** not accepted **Closed** late Apr to mid-June, mid-Oct to early Dec
Proprietors Senoner family

Trentino-Alto Adige

Mountain hotel, Sesto

Tirol

The little town of Sesto (or Sexten) is one of the prettiest in the region, and the surrounding area must be one of the most beautiful parts of the Dolomites. The Berghotel Tirol is a recently constructed chalet, with dark wood balconies overlooking classic alpine scenery: a gentle valley dotted with chalets, a church spire in the foreground, and in the distance, the jagged peaks which are so characteristic of the area. In summer, there are walking trails; in winter you can ski. The comfortable, pine-furnished hotel is run with great hospitality and efficiency by the Holzer family. For self-caterers, there is an apartment-house next door.
Nearby Cortina d'Ampezzo (44 km).

Moso, 39030 Sesto, Bolzano **Tel** (0474) 710386 **Fax** (0474) 710455 **Location** in Moso, 2 km SE of Sesto, which is on the SS355, 44 km NE of Cortina; ample parking **Meals** breakfast, lunch, dinner **Prices** half board L97,000–L157,000 per person; in standard double L94,000–L144,000 per person; breakfast included **Rooms** 45 double and twin, single and suites, all with bath or shower; all rooms have phone, TV, hairdrier **Facilities** sitting room, dining room, bar, sauna/solarium, lift, terrace **Credit cards** not accepted **Children** welcome **Disabled** access difficult **Pets** accepted **Closed** Easter to mid-May, Oct to Christmas **Proprietors** Holzer family

Castle restaurant-with-rooms, Tirolo

Schloss Thurnstein

You must negotiate 4 kilometres of tortuous hairpin bends to reach this grey stone edifice built in 1200 as a defence tower for nearby Castel Tirolo. The reputation of the restaurant is well-established, and chef Toni Bauer is a larger-than-life figure, passionate about unpretentious cooking using the freshest of ingredients. Activity revolves around the series of dining rooms, and the two terraces (one on each side of the building – ideal for juggling sun and shade) have spectacular views. The comfortable bedrooms are in a nearby annexe; some have separate sitting areas.
Nearby Merano (5 km); Bolzano (28 km); Castel Tirolo (2 km).

Tirolo, 39019 Merano, Bolzano **Tel** (0473) 220255 **Fax** (0473) 220558 **Location** 5 km N of Merano on mountainside with limited parking **Meals** breakfast, lunch, dinner **Prices** rooms L65,000–L162,000; standard double L106,000–L162,000; breakfast included; dinner from L40,000 **Rooms** 10; 8 double (one twin), 2 single, all with bath or shower; all rooms have phone **Facilities** restaurants, terraces, sitting room **Credit cards** MC, V **Children** accepted **Disabled** not suitable **Pets** not accepted **Closed** early to mid-July, mid-Nov to mid-Mar **Proprietors** Bauer family

Trentino-Alto Adige

Mountain restaurant-with-rooms, Villandro

Ansitz Zum Steinbock

Villandro is a pretty mountain village, and Ansitz Zum Steinbock stands at its centre. An imposing 18thC building, it looks rather forbidding from the outside, but the jolly terrace (where you can eat in warm weather) is a clue to the welcoming, typically Tyrolean interior – fresh and simple, with pine-clad or white-painted walls, pretty fabrics for curtains and tablecloths and rustic furniture and artefacts here and there. You will eat well: the restaurant is highly regarded locally for its regional cooking. Bedrooms are beamed, with modern pine beds and plump white duvets.

Nearby Bressanone (13 km); Val Gardena; Bolzano (28 km).

San Stefano 38, 39040
Villandro, Bolzano
Tel (0472) 843111
Fax (0472) 843468
Location off SS12, Chiusa exit, 28 km NE of Bolzano; in village with parking
Meals breakfast, lunch, dinner
Prices rooms L55,000– L130,000; standard double L120,000; breakfast included; dinner from L50,000 **Rooms** 15 double and twin, 1 single, all with bath or shower; all rooms have phone, TV **Facilities** dining rooms, terrace **Credit cards** AE, MC, V **Children** accepted **Disabled** access difficult **Pets** accepted **Closed** mid-Jan to mid-Mar; restaurant Mon **Proprietors** Signor and Signora Kirchbaumer

Index of hotel names

In this index hotels are arranged in order of the most distinctive part of their names. Very common prefixes such as 'Il' and 'La' are placed after the name. More descriptive words such as 'Castello', 'Locanda' and 'Villa' are included in the name.

Index of hotel names

Index of hotel locations

In this index hotels are arranged by the name of the city, town or village they are in or near. Hotels located in a very small village may be indexed under a larger place nearby. An index by hotel name precedes this one.